BISHOP OLMSTED
ON LIFE, FAITH, AND LEADERSHIP

TEPEYAC LEADERSHIP SERIES

BISHOP OLMSTED
ON LIFE, FAITH, AND LEADERSHIP

TEPEYAC LEADERSHIP SERIES

TLI
PUBLISHING
Phoenix, AZ

About the Tepeyac Leadership Series

Tepeyac Leadership, Inc. (TLI) is a non-profit organization dedicated to civic leadership development for lay Catholic professionals around the globe. The Tepeyac Leadership Series is part of TLI's mission to deliver civic leadership development to lay Catholics in the U.S. and beyond. TLI offers a catalyst development experience that equips lay Catholics to become virtuous leaders, influence the culture and serve the common good. Learn more at TLIprogram.org.

Cristofer Pereyra is a native of Peru. Married and the father of four, in 2014, he was asked by Bishop Thomas Olmsted to serve the Diocese of Phoenix. In 2018, executing Bishop Olmsted's vision, Pereyra developed the innovative diocesan program Tepeyac Leadership Initiative. The early fruit from its graduates and a deep love for the Church inspired Pereyra to found the global Catholic apostolate, Tepeyac Leadership, Inc.

Laurie Strom is a Deacon's wife, grandmother, and a former Executive VP & COO of SAE Industry Technologies Consortia and Honeywell Aerospace Director, where she managed engineering teams in multiple countries. Now, she is a mentor, coach, writer, and photographer - praising God and finding science and faith beautifully intertwined. There is beauty in a job well done.

Cover Design: Maria Fernanda Hernandez

Scripture verses contained herein are from the New American Bible Revised Edition, United States Conference of Catholic Bishops (https://bible.usccb.org/bible)

ISBN: 979-8-9907711-0-9

Printed in the United States of America

Dedication

This book is dedicated to the first seven cohorts of the TLI program –
2018 through 2024. May they continue to deepen their faith,
prosper in their professional pursuits, and become the virtuous
leaders they are meant to be.

"O Mother, strengthen the faith of our brothers and sisters in the
laity, so that in every field of social, professional, cultural and
political life, they may act in accordance with the truth and the law
brought by your son to mankind." (St. John Paul II 1979)

Hail Mary
St. Juan Diego, Pray for us.

TABLE OF CONTENTS

(para. x) indicates the applicable paragraph number.

TABLE OF CONTENTS (CONT.)

(para. x) indicates the applicable paragraph number.

TABLE OF CONTENTS (CONT.)

(para. x) indicates the applicable paragraph number.

FOREWORD

Courageous prophet or anti-Francis culture warrior?
The Bishop Olmsted I knew was simply a pastor.

It was late. I was the editor of a diocesan newspaper, and I had logged extra hours that day to prepare the latest issue to go to press. It must have been between 10 and 11 p.m. by the time I took the elevator down to the subterranean garage at the chancery.

I was surprised to hear boisterous chatter when the elevator doors opened. I peeked around the corner to see Sergio, the security guard, prattling on. Now, Sergio did not fit any security guard stereotypes. He was timid, soft-spoken and did not make a lot of eye contact. Bit of a conflict-averse wallflower.

I had worked with Sergio for years but had never seen him this animated. He was smiling with his eyes wide, emphasizing his words with his hands and laughing. It seemed like the person he was speaking to was having a tough time getting a word in. I peeked a little further around the corner and saw Sergio speaking with Bishop Thomas J. Olmsted.

Bishop Olmsted is retiring as the ordinary of the Diocese of Phoenix. Pope Francis accepted his resignation recently and appointed Bishop John P. Dolan, San Diego's auxiliary bishop, to succeed him. I haven't worked for Bishop Olmsted since 2013. Still, of his more than 18 years as Bishop of Phoenix, I was there for nine.

If you don't live in Phoenix and you happen to have heard of Bishop Olmsted, there is a good chance it has to do with St. Joseph's Hospital. Bishop Olmsted gained national attention after informing a religious sister of her excommunication for her involvement with an abortion at the hospital. Eventually, in 2009, he stripped the hospital of its Catholic status.

You may have also heard about how in 2004 he asked nine priests and one religious brother to remove their names from the "Phoenix Declaration," a public statement organized by the group *No Longer Silent* and signed by Christian clergy in support of "gay, lesbian, bisexual and transgendered persons."

Bishop Olmsted made news again in 2018, after Archbishop Carlo Maria Viganò, the former papal nuncio to the United States, published a lengthy testimony alleging a cover-up regarding former Cardinal Theodore McCarrick's long history of sexual abuse. A few days later, Bishop Olmsted issued a statement calling Archbishop Viganò "a man of truthfulness, faith and integrity." While Bishop Olmsted admitted having no knowledge of the information disclosed by Archbishop Viganò, he said the claims should be "investigated thoroughly."

I know a number of people have felt hurt by Bishop Olmsted's decisions. I have myself. I credit the Dominicans for keeping me Catholic in college, so when the bishop removed them from the Newman Center at Arizona State University, I felt like I should quit my position at the diocese. I was crushed more recently when I heard the diocese would stop publishing The Catholic Sun, the diocesan paper where I began my career. During my time as a diocesan employee, I understood or agreed with certain decisions, but I did not understand and disagreed with others.

Some friends of mine believe Bishop Olmsted is a saint and a prophet and praise his most controversial decisions as courageous. Other friends believe him to be too rigid and dogmatic, a "culture warrior" who, they believe, resists the Francis pontificate.

When you know someone only from afar and not through the culture of encounter to which Pope Francis has called all of us, it can be easy to villainize or even commodify other human beings. I understand Bishop Olmsted differently precisely because of proximity. I witnessed interactions that complicate the storyline of a rigid shepherd that some put forth.

I first met Bishop Olmsted when he sat in on my second interview to get the position at The Catholic Sun. During that interview, I mentioned that Rosemary Radford Ruether sat on my master's thesis committee. I thought Bishop Olmsted's eyes were going to pop out. But they hired me anyway.

And I often think of that late night where I found him talking—or listening really—to Sergio: how he gave this security guard his undivided attention so late at night. When I drove by them—you know, hoping the big boss might see me working late—the bishop didn't even look up. That's the way Bishop Olmsted talks to people.

After Masses, he is the guy who stands outside in his vestments when it's blazing hot, spending as long as it takes until everyone who wants to speak with him has a chance. I have rarely, if ever, seen him rush one of these casual conversations. When you talk to him, you feel like you are the center of his universe. (It was a little frustrating, frankly, when all I wanted was to get a quick quote from him after Mass.)

His predecessor, Bishop Thomas J. O'Brien, built the current chancery building, which has a separate priest dining room where the priests were to eat lunch together each day. At least, that was the plan. Under Bishop Olmsted's leadership, the dining room is rarely used. Instead, during my time there, everyone ate together in the cafeteria.

That included Bishop Olmsted. If there was a person sitting alone, he would often join that person. And he would remember what you shared with him and bring it up the next time he picked your table— or perhaps if he ran into you in the hall. (Not the elevator, though, because Bishop Olmsted always took the stairs.) When I worked there, he knew everyone's names. And I could never tell if he had favorites.

There is (or used to be) a "bishop's residence," located in a well-to-do Phoenix neighborhood. Bishop Olmsted never lived there. Instead, he lives in a small room in the Sts. Simon and Jude Cathedral rectory. The cathedral is nice, don't get me wrong. But it is certainly not located in a wealthy neighborhood. The bishop told me once that he lived in the rectory because he liked community life and wanted to be in relationship with others.

He took over in Phoenix at what must have felt like an impossible time for the diocese. His predecessor, Bishop O'Brien, had resigned days after fleeing the scene of a fatal car accident. Before that, Bishop O'Brien had signed an agreement with the county attorney's office in which he admitted to protecting priests accused of child sexual abuse.

"I really don't know why I was asked," Bishop Olmsted told The Catholic Advance, the Wichita diocesan paper, at the time of his appointment to Phoenix in 2003. "I think it would be linked with the fact that the Diocese of Wichita is a really good diocese. And because of that, it looks like I'm doing O.K. as a bishop."

Through it all, it always seemed like Bishop Olmsted stayed in touch with his upbringing on a farm on the Kansas-Nebraska border. He grew up with five brothers and sisters, and his family would heat up old catalogs on the stove to keep their feet warm in bed.

After his ordination as a priest, Bishop Olmsted joined the Jesus Caritas priestly fraternity, which is inspired by St. Charles de Foucauld, a French priest who lived in the Sahara and sought to be a brother to everyone. It is because of this saint that Bishop Olmsted keeps a statue of the child Jesus in his office and near his bed.

"A lot of times those who do not know Christ will be frightened of the crucifix," the bishop told me years ago for a profile I wrote on his 10-year anniversary in Phoenix. "But no one is frightened of a baby."

While I worked for him, Bishop Olmsted made it a point to regularly visit the Native American reservations in the area. On Christmas Eve, he would typically celebrate the midnight Mass at the cathedral; on Christmas Day, he would celebrate the morning Mass at one of the local prisons, before heading to the airport to visit his family.

Bishop Olmsted never struck me as a person driven by an agenda, other than what he believes to be the teaching of the Catholic Church. To find out what that teaching is, I believe he would point you to the *Catechism of the Catholic Church* and the Bible, among other sources. Some might consider that a simplistic answer, but whatever it is, I never thought it was driven by personal ego.

In this time of polarization—both in our society and in our Church—can we learn from those with whom we disagree? Perhaps understanding ourselves as "progressive" or "conservative" might help us identify the differences that need to be bridged. But when such categories are used as barriers to communion, they are deeply un-Christian.

4

In so many ways, I have come to deeply admire Bishop Olmsted. Prayer is central to his life. He lives simply. He cares deeply for others, including the marginalized. He gives his undivided attention to those who wish to speak with him. (My wife would love it if I were more like that.)

I believe Bishop Olmsted will enjoy his retirement. He will certainly have more time for prayer and hiking in the desert, one of his favorite pastimes. I understand he will be in residence at one of the parishes in the diocese. And I imagine he will be tapped to do confirmations now and then. But in some ways, he'll focus more on his priestly ministry. And, it seems to me, a priest is what he has always wanted to be.

By J.D. Long-García
Written for America, June 15, 2022. (García 2022)

INTRODUCTION

Our life in Christ is not one of "do's and don'ts," but an adventure in authentic freedom. Embrace that freedom in order to place your life at the service of Christ, beginning in your home and radiating into the world. (Olmsted, 2015, Into the Breach)

The Tepeyac Leadership Series was started to offer contemporary models of lay Catholic leadership. While the objective of the series and its intended focus is to showcase lay Catholic leaders, the publisher decided for the first book in the series to feature the clergyman who founded the movement it represents, the Most Reverend Thomas J. Olmsted, Bishop Emeritus of Phoenix.

This book is a collaboration between Cristofer Pereyra, the journalist who held the intimate conversation that laid the foundation for the book, and Laurie Strom, the editor. Not all the questions in the book were from the interview. Follow-up questions were sent to Bishop Olmsted, and his responses were incorporated into the book.

Bishop Olmsted: on life, faith, and leadership seeks to capture the life and wisdom of a shepherd dedicated to his flock. It was born out of admiration and desire to inspire future generations through Bishop Olmsted's example. All proceeds from the sale of the book go to funding the mission of TLI.

The book is structured to give the reader an insight into three concrete areas in the life of Bishop Olmsted. With the aid of the table of contents, the reader may jump into the area or questions he wants to learn about first and explore the rest at his own pace.

Thank you for your interest in the life of Bishop Olmsted and your support of TLI. Thank you for the time you will dedicate to reading this book. We hope you find in its pages much inspiration to nurture your own life, faith, and leadership.

Part 1

Life

I was aware from the beginning that God was very real, that our life was a gift from Him and that we constantly lived in His presence. (para. 5)

Stay firmly on the path that puts Jesus first in your life and facilitates your keeping Him first. Keep the eyes of your heart fixed on Jesus. (cf. Heb. 12:2) (para. 240)

---

1. Cristofer: *Thank you for accepting to be part of the Tepeyac Leadership series, Bishop Olmsted. I'd like to start with the historical context in which you were born. Tell me about the era of American history you were born into. What was it like?*

2. Bishop Olmsted: It was right after the Second World War when I was born, January 21st, 1947, to Margaret Helen and Patrick Olmsted. It was a time when the United States was becoming aware of being an international leader. The Second World War was over, and that dimension on the national and international levels was beginning to impact the Church in the United States. We began to think of ourselves as having a responsibility in the larger context, beyond just ourselves locally. That wasn't something I was aware of at the time because I was born and raised on a little farm in Kansas. It was a very simple life.

3. I was raised in a home that was very Catholic, where to pray was as natural as breathing. I was born into a stable family with two older brothers and three younger sisters. We were the only Catholics in the area. It was a mostly non-Catholic area; most people would have been Christian but not Catholic. Quite a lot of anti-Catholicism was present in that era in that section [of the country] where I was.

4. Cristofer: *Please describe your household a little bit more, Bishop. What are your earliest memories from when you were a child?*

5. Bishop Olmsted: Well, I was aware from the beginning that God was very real, that our life was a gift from Him and that we constantly lived in His presence. So, we prayed at every meal. We knelt in front of the dresser in my parents' bedroom and prayed every evening. We would pray the Rosary in the evenings during May and October. So, prayer was just a natural part of it.

6. Since my brothers and I were all just one year apart, there was the constant effort to love my brothers and to also relate with all the members of the farm community around us as good neighbors. We went to Mass on Sundays, nine miles away. It was a little tiny mission church, and we had Mass on Sundays when the priest was able to get there, and when we were able to get there because the roads were not good, they were mostly dirt. So, it was a very simple life.

7. Cristofer: *So, this was a mission?*

8. Bishop Olmsted: It was a mission church, yes. The pastor lived near the main church and drove to this church on Sundays.

9. Cristofer: *The Faith was obviously the central part of your family life, but what else did you do? What do you remember doing for fun with your siblings?*

10. Bishop Olmsted: We were always enjoying the outdoors. On the farm, whenever it rained in the summer, we would go fishing. That was one of the ways we provided food for ourselves. So, we did a lot of fishing, hunting, especially in the winter, and trapping. We would trap minks, muskrats, beavers, coyotes, and all kinds of animals like that. The trapping was for pelts that we sold.

11. Cristofer: *You were a member of the 4-H youth program when you were young, correct? What were your favorite projects? What can young people learn from organizations such as 4-H that can help them later in life?*

12. Bishop Olmsted: My brothers and sisters and I were all members of 4-H. My projects were "market pigs," gardening and cooking. One especially helpful part of 4-H was learning how to conduct meetings according to Robert's Rules. Also enjoyable were Square Dancing, singing, and participating in activities and exhibits at the county fair.

13. So, we really lived very close to the land, to the farm. But we also were very involved with baseball in the summer. And then, once we got into high school, with basketball, as well. But our nearest neighbors were a mile away. So, our own family had a big impact on my life because of the - not isolation but - distance from others.

14. Cristofer: *Your family was your world, basically.*

15. Bishop Olmsted: In many ways, yes! Now, our relatives close to us were all non-Catholic and anti-Catholic because my father was a convert. My grandparents lived just two miles away. My grandfather was very open, but my grandmother was anti-Catholic. My dad had one sister who lived fifteen miles away, and they were not Catholic. So, we were very conscious of being different.

16. Cristofer: *When did you make your parents' Faith your own? Having grown up in a Catholic household, at what point did you decide to make it yours?*

17. Bishop Olmsted: I would say it was mine always, partly because almost all our neighbors were non-Catholic and some anti-Catholic. So, I was conscious of that. When I started going to a little school, for example, two miles away, I either rode a bicycle or a horse. There were only four or five families that made up that school. We were the only Catholics. If we came to school after going to early Mass for Ash Wednesday and had the ashes on our foreheads, we obviously were different. They would want to know about that. There was no support from any of them for the Catholic Faith. There were more questions and a kind of uneasiness with us.

18. There were other families in the Faith that lived at some distance from us and drove to the one church we went to in Nebraska. It was wonderful getting together with them, but that was not on a daily basis.

19. So, there was no major switch in that regard. I can remember thinking of being a priest when I was four or five, and that never really went away. There was never a crisis time in that at all.

20. Cristofer: *I've heard the stories of priests saying that it is a calling. They say you hear a calling, and that's how you know it's from God.*

Tell me about the evolution of your vocation and the different thresholds.

21. Bishop Olmsted: I'd say a couple of things made it real for me. One was that I always had a fascination with the Sacred Liturgy, the Eucharist, and with the Stations of the Cross during Lent. There was something about the great mystery of Christ being present with us that just deeply attracted me. I have always been fascinated by Catholic churches and the Blessed Sacrament. If ever I was near a Catholic church, it was like a magnet that drew me to go in, stop and pray. That's true to this day, but that really started when I was a young child.

22. The other part of it would be that I could tell the Faith made a real difference in our family. There was a peacefulness and unity in our family which I didn't feel when I was with other families. Even though we had neighbors and relatives who were anti-Catholic, my mom and dad never spoke negatively of them at all. There was never an articulation about "Isn't this bad?" or anything like that. So, reflecting back as I grew older, I thought, this is striking, such patience with others! My parents explained things to us in a way that would never sound negative. One example is that I was named after my grandfather on my dad's side. He was Tom Olmsted. He never had been raised in the Faith at all. My mother always spoke very highly of him because he was a man of character. He was always true to his word, but it didn't come from his faith. There were ways they [my mother and father] always found to say positive things about others.

23. Cristofer: *It sounds like you really had what Saint Josemaría Escrivá calls a bright and cheerful home. Yet there are always struggles and suffering; it is an inescapable aspect of the human experience. Tell me about one or two in your early life.*

24. Bishop Olmsted: One of the struggles that we all have is the death of someone that we love. I was named after both my grandparents, Grandpa Jim and Grandpa Thomas. (James is my middle name.) Both of them died when I was outside of the United States, so this was a little later.

25. In my second year in college seminary, while working in the missions in Mexico, my grandfather died on my mother's side of the family. I remember feeling so alone with that sorrow because I was a long way away from the family. Going to Christ in the Eucharist and in prayer was very comforting, and it gave me a sense of where to bring the sorrow in my own heart. I was not able to get back; I didn't even know about his death for a couple of weeks because of where I was working in Mexico.

26. When my other grandfather died, which would have been about five years later, I was in Rome. I remember receiving a message that was just written out that someone had called from the United States to let me know my grandfather had died. I remember reading that note, walking to the chapel, and spending an hour and a half just weeping in front of the Blessed Sacrament. It was very consoling, and at the end of that, there was a real sense of Christ being very near to me. So, those were kind of crises, but they were always linked closely with my faith in Christ.

27. **Cristofer**: *These are painful moments in life, but these are natural events.*

28. **Bishop Olmsted:** They are.

29. **Cristofer:** *So, you can't point out a time when there were major struggles? It seems to me the environment in your life was so positive and faith-filled that perhaps you were not even aware of it, but I'm sure at one point your parents struggled with money, like most families, right? Being a farming family, were the crops ruined at some point? Did anything like that happen?*

30. **Bishop Olmsted:** Yes, they did. We had hailstorms that would destroy the crops completely - the row crops that we planted. But it was interesting the way our parents described it, "God is with us. We will get through this." Because we lived very simply, if we didn't have any crops to sell, we still had plenty to eat because we raised chickens, pigs and cattle; we always had the cows we milked. And we raised horses.

31. So, we just lived more simply. We always lived rather simply, actually. So, in many ways, I didn't think of that [struggle]. I'm sure

my mother and father must have felt that, but we children never did. As a child, I wasn't very aware of that at all because they really did trust that God was going to get us through these things. They didn't have to tell us that very often because we could see how they were doing it.

32. Cristofer: *You didn't see anxiety?*

33. Bishop Olmsted: I do remember one time that was very striking on my dad's part. He was a convert before he married my mother, but as a child, he wasn't a Catholic. I remember one of his friends [and family], who lived about 10 miles away, were out on the river fishing. They got caught up in a net, and they all drowned in the river. I remember it was a huge sorrow for my dad. It left a deep impression on me because you can't explain it; it's hard to talk about that in a way that explains how God could allow this to happen. There were three sons, and just like that, all four of them were dead.

34. It was easy to imagine because we had three sons in my family, and we often fished in the creeks ourselves. So, my father, especially with his own sorrow, was amazing. Everything we did, we brought to the Lord. So, it didn't hang over us for a long time. My father probably was dealing with it more than I was aware of because, certainly, the initial shock was very, very difficult for him.

35. Cristofer: *Bishop, who were one or two of the most influential people in your family?*

36. Bishop Olmsted: Both my father and mother, certainly, in the way they lived their lives in the presence of God. My father was a convert, but his dad, sister and mom were not. His mother and sister were anti-Catholic, but he lived his life so grateful for his Catholic Faith. That was evident in the way that we went to Mass every Sunday, and every other Sunday, we would go to Confession before Mass. There was just a rhythm about life that fit with a rhythm of nature that we looked forward to.

37. You might say my mother's faith was more informed because she had gone to nurse's training in a Catholic hospital, and she read more than my father did. He had never gone beyond high school in terms of studies. He could have learned more if he had the opportunity, but

he did not have that. He gladly just accepted he was called to be a farmer, and he enjoyed farming.

38. Cristofer: *Tell me briefly about his story of conversion. I recall that was sort of the way he could marry your mother.*

39. Bishop Olmsted: It was, yes. They met when they were juniors in high school; that's when my mom moved from a Catholic school in the same little town. They only had a Catholic school up to the sophomore level in high school, so then, when she went to the public school, they met. About November, my dad walked up to my mom and said, "I'm taking you to Midnight Mass." So that was his first proposal for a date, and it was an unusual way! I said, "Mom, what did you say?" She replied, "I said, 'You're doing what?' and he said, 'I would like to take you to Midnight Mass!'"

40. He'd never been inside a Catholic church. His mother was anti-Catholic. Of course, he was a teenager, so there may have been some, you know, kind of sketchy things there… But his first encounter with the Catholic Faith in a church was Midnight Mass with the beauty of the music and the beauty of the Sacred Liturgy. He never told me about that, but you could, as I look back, see he really treasured those mysteries of our Faith, which are so different when you're raised Protestant, where it's just the Word of God that you have. Actually, they didn't go to church on the other side of the family, so he didn't really have much of that at all.

41. So, their first date was at Midnight Mass, and he continued to really like this young woman. She went off to nurses training with classmates when she finished high school, and he stayed home. It was during World War II and farmers were raising food for overseas. They [the local farmers] were heavily involved, so he stayed home on the farm working. He did not get drafted because of a heart murmur.

42. When he proposed marriage to my mom, she said, "You know it's important for me that we both be Catholic." He said, "I know. I already joined the Church." So, he had done that on his own. Without telling his parents, he'd sought out a Catholic priest and taken instructions. He obviously was really taken by the Faith that he observed in the liturgy and in my mom.

43. Cristofer: *Remind me, your heritage is Irish?*

44. Bishop Olmsted: My mother is Irish, yes.

45. Cristofer: *On your father's side?*

46. Bishop Olmsted: On my father's side, the name is Norwegian. So, there would be Norwegian there, but I'm not sure what else there might have been.

47. Cristofer: *Let's go to your vocation again, Bishop. So, from an early age it began manifesting. At what point was it clear that this is the path, and I'm going to follow it?*

48. Bishop Olmsted: As I say often, I really felt called to be a priest, but I didn't talk to others about that until my senior year in high school. I was asked by the priest in the town where I went to high school, which was a little rural high school, to come down and see him after school one day. When I went, he said, "Did you ever think about being a Catholic priest?" and I said, "Yes." He said, "Well, I think you might be called to be a priest." He just explained very simply, "God often calls those who come from a family where the Faith is alive. I have visited your home before and noticed that you pray together and that the Catholic Faith is evident throughout your home. I know that you do well in school academically. I see that you're very involved with athletics. So, in other words, you have the intellectual ability, you have the physical capacity, and you come from a place where the Faith is alive; that's usually where a call can be heard and accepted." He gave me a little book to read, and he said, "Why don't you come back next week, and we'll talk about this." I remember the book was about the vocation to be a priest, and written for someone about my age, a senior in high school.

49. Cristofer: *What happened after that?*

50. Bishop Olmsted: Well, he said, "If you're going to be a priest, you have to decide whether you want to be a priest in a religious community or in a diocese." He explained the difference, and said, "Your situation in terms of diocese is a little complicated. I'm a priest of the Archdiocese of Kansas City, and you've been going to Mass in Nebraska, which is the Diocese of Lincoln. You have to decide which of these you would go to." I said, "Well, the only place I've really gone to Mass has been on the Nebraska side." So, he said, "Well, you'll have to talk to the priest there then."

51. It took me a little while to ask the priest there [in Nebraska] if I could see him after Mass. When I did, and I told him that I thought God might be calling me to be a priest, he said, "I think your brother would make a good priest." So, he wasn't really excited... I'm sure he was thinking of my oldest brother. We had all served at Mass and been active in the Church. Anyway, it just so happened that a week later, there was a retreat being offered by the Diocese of Lincoln for those who were juniors and seniors in high school. So, he said, "The next time, you may want to do this." I went there immediately. I was sure that's what God was calling me to be.

52. Cristofer: *Your story is so different, Bishop, from others that I've heard. In others, there's not such a big conviction. In yours, there was such conviction!*

53. But I do have a question. You probably didn't imagine you were going to be a bishop. What type of priest did young Thomas want to be? You probably were enthusiastic about it, imagining yourself as a priest. What was the ideal that you hoped for?

54. Bishop Olmsted: Well, the ideal I had was [based on] the only priests I knew who lived and served in small rural areas because that's what I had seen. I could see they were happy as priests, and I could see what a difference it made in the lives of the people they were with, especially in an area that was largely non-Catholic. So, that's what I thought of because that's all I knew.

55. Now, our home did have quite a few books, and I read quite a few on the lives of saints and that kind of thing. So, I was also drawn to missionary activity; that was another thing I thought about seriously. Father Miguel Pro was someone I read about in high school. His courage in facing persecution in Mexico inspired me to follow his example.

56. Cristofer: *So, it wasn't immediately clear that you were going to be a diocesan priest?*

57. Bishop Olmsted: I thought about the idea of being a missionary. In fact, even the very first priest asked me that question. He said, "You also have to think about whether you want to be a missionary or not." I said, "Well, that is something," because I had read about the Maryknoll Fathers and Brothers, as well, and was struck by that. So, I asked him, "Why did you decide to be a diocesan priest?" The priest answered, "Because our farm was nearest to a church in a rural area of central Kansas, I felt called to serve the people there in in the Archdiocese of Kansas City." What he said made sense to me, so I followed a similar course.

58. Cristofer: *How did becoming a priest and then a bishop impact the rest of your family – your brothers and sisters?*

59. Bishop Olmsted: When my parents were asked whether they were proud to have a son become a bishop, they replied, "We are proud of all our children." That wonderful response affirmed the vocation of all my siblings. It made it easy to love and encourage one another and not have to deal with jealousy or rivalry. We are all grateful to God for mom and dad.

60. Cristofer: *So now, take me through your ecclesiastical appointments. Walk me through from your ordination to becoming seminary rector and from becoming Bishop of Wichita to Bishop of Phoenix. Walk me through how all of that evolved and how the news of it came about. What it was like every time you were surprised with how God was calling you to serve the Church, starting from ordination and your first appointment, all the way to bishop in Phoenix. Take your time.*

61. Bishop Olmsted: Okay. I entered seminary right out of high school. The bishop sent me to Denver, so I was there for my first four years of college seminary.

62. It actually was a time of great turmoil in the Church because it was the very end of the Second Vatican Council. In 1965, I started college seminary and continued until 1969. Great turbulence was happening in the larger Church at that time.

63. Cristofer: *How did that turbulence affect you in the seminary?*

64. Bishop Olmsted: It affected me after the second year, 1967. Priest faculty members started leaving the priesthood about two or three each year during the last two years I was there. It was puzzling to me because this was a much bigger world than I had grown up in. I was totally in awe of the rich intellectual heritage of the Catholic Church. I'd never been in a Catholic institution because I was raised in a very non-Catholic rural area. So, I became a student librarian for all my years in seminary because I was fascinated by that [legacy]. I couldn't understand why these priests were leaving.

65. I would read about these stories [of priests leaving], but they didn't touch me that much personally. None of them were priests I really had gotten close to. My spiritual directors were all fine during that era, the ones that were closest to me in that sense.

66. Then, I was sent to Rome for my last four years, from 1969 to 1973. It was far more turbulent over there. The tumultuous issuance of *Humanae Vitae* was on July 25th, 1968. (Paul VI 1968) So, it was a year later when I got to Rome. There was great turmoil in the theological community.

67. Cristofer: *This was all before you were ordained?*

68. Bishop Olmsted: This was all before I was ordained, yes, and by this time, I'm studying theology and becoming aware of this. There was a lot of dissent among faculty members, especially in Rome. I had professors like Josef Fuchs, who dissented from the Church's teaching of moral theology, and so I became aware of all this kind of turmoil. Also, within the student body in Rome, there was a lot of turmoil as well. But, partly because of my background, it didn't deeply disturb me within. It made me really try to figure out, "What in the world is happening here?"

69. Cristofer: *You were right at peace when you got ordained!*

70. Bishop Olmsted: Yes, I was always at peace. It didn't frighten me in that way. So, I got ordained in Rome in St. Peter's Basilica on July 2nd, 1973. So, that was 49 years ago!

71. Cristofer: *Since then, you have traveled and served in several countries. Where is your favorite place to visit?*

72. Bishop Olmsted: Having lived in Italy, there are many villages and cities there, many associated with great saints, where I love to spend time – such as Assisi, Siena, Rome, Pisa, and Castel Gandolfo. Making a retreat in Assisi prior to my ordination as a deacon [a level prior to ordination as a priest] made a deep impression on me and confirmed my desire to serve Jesus for the rest of my life.

73. Cristofer: *Where did you study in Rome?*

74. Bishop Olmsted: I lived at the North American College, and I studied at the Pontifical Gregorian University, which is the Jesuit university there.

75. Then [after priestly ordination], I came back to the Diocese of Lincoln, and my assignment was at the cathedral parish in Lincoln, Nebraska. It was a large parish with a Catholic school.

76. Cristofer: *What is the name of the cathedral where you did your first assignment?*

77. Bishop Olmsted: The name was Cathedral of the Risen Christ. There were four priests in the rectory: the pastor, the vicar general of the diocese, and two associate priests - I was one of those. I was teaching very heavily. I was teaching fifth and sixth grade religion every day. I was teaching kindergarten, first, second, and fourth grade one day a week, and I was teaching juniors every day at a high school. So, a lot of teaching right away. It was good because I was now using what I had been studying all these years. Being thrown into the classroom where you're getting asked all kinds of questions, especially by the juniors in the high school, was a good challenge for me. I was also asked to serve as the master of ceremonies for the bishop during those three years. So, on a lot of Sundays and weekends, I would be traveling with him or assisting him in that way.

78. Cristofer: *You were asked to be the master of ceremonies for the bishop? Why do you think they asked you?*

79. Bishop Olmsted: The bishop would come to the cathedral every Saturday night to hear Confessions. That was a habit of his. He wanted to show the importance of Confession. So, he got to know the priests that were there [at the cathedral]. He had always chosen his master of ceremonies from the priests who were assigned there. The other priest who was there had been ordained for nine or ten years, and he didn't want to be the master of ceremonies. He served once, and he did it in such a poor way that the bishop never asked him again!

80. Cristofer: *Which bishop was this?*

81. Bishop Olmsted: This was Bishop Glennon P. Flavin, an Irish American bishop who was originally a priest in St. Louis, Missouri, and came to the diocese in 1967. He was a blessing to me because he had a really strong conviction about the teachings of the Church being something that we had to be loyal to and faithful to. That was really good because I had come from this wild intellectual kind of turmoil that was happening in Rome. He was aware of that, but he wasn't buying into it at all. Since I traveled with him a lot and emceed with him, we had many conversations during that time. We got along very well. We both loved sports. He had been a really good athlete, especially playing soccer. I always played a lot of sports as well. So, we could talk about who our favorite team was and that kind of thing, but we also could talk about the Faith. After three years, he asked me to go back to Rome and do doctoral studies, partly because he didn't have a lot of young priests with doctoral degrees.

82. Cristofer: *What were these doctoral studies?*

83. Bishop Olmsted: Canon Law. We had a Canon Lawyer who was already 68 and no other. The little diocese really needed someone else to study Canon Law. I had studied in Rome, so I already knew Italian and Latin, the languages that I needed for that. So, that's how I went back to studies three years after being ordained in 1976.

84. Cristofer: *How did you go from doctoral studies to working for Pope John Paul II?*

85. Bishop Olmsted: I finished my doctoral studies in 1979. John Paul II was elected in 1978 in October. And in March, I was asked if I would be part of the Secretariat of State to assist him.

86. Cristofer: *You were asked by who?*

87. Bishop Olmsted: I was asked by an official of the Secretariat of State.

88. Cristofer: *You were studying for your doctorate?*

89. Bishop Olmsted: Yes, I was studying for my doctorate in Canon Law when John Paul II was elected on October 16th, 1978. It was evident after he went to Mexico, his first trip outside of Italy, that he was going to be traveling the world a lot. He was going to need assistance with the English language because much of the world was speaking English then. French was no longer the major international language. They needed priests to assist the Secretariat of State, whose first language was English but who could work in three or four other languages, especially Italian and Latin. They should also have a doctorate or be very close to finishing their doctorate, which is where I was at that time.

90. Cristofer: *You were a good fit. You were the profile.*

91. Bishop Olmsted: Yes, I was, but they didn't really know me well. I don't know where they got this information. They might have just asked the university if they had any English speakers who were finishing their doctorates - that kind of thing.

92. Cristofer: *What happened after that?*

93. Bishop Olmsted: Well, I said no to the Secretariat of State. I said, "I don't think it's fair to my diocese. The priest we have there is already over 70. It's a small diocese. There are not many resources." So, I was told, "Well, don't you think your bishop is the one who should make that decision?" And I said, "Yes, I do. If he says yes, I'll say yes. But I would like to be able to write to him and tell him I didn't ask for this. I'm willing to do whatever you want me to do, but I didn't ask for this, so it's not something that would break my heart if it doesn't happen."

94. Cristofer: *So, I assume the bishop said, go ahead, Thomas.*

95. Bishop Olmsted: Well, actually, he wrote a letter. When he got the [request] letter, he sat down and wrote back, "No, we just don't have any; you should choose a large diocese that has more priests and people with doctorates."

96. Cristofer: *He concurred with you?*

97. Bishop Olmsted: He did. But he didn't send the letter, and he couldn't sleep that night. He kept thinking, "How can I say no to the successor of St. Peter?" So, he got up the next morning, tore that letter up, and wrote one giving me permission to do it.

98. Cristofer: *Wow. He wrote a letter supporting your instinct that this was not a good idea. He couldn't sleep, and then the next day, he tore it up and wrote a different one supporting it?*

99. Bishop Olmsted: Yes.

100. Cristofer: *What was his letter? Do you remember reading his letter?*

101. Bishop Olmsted: Well, he showed it to me. He said, "I'm giving permission for Father Olmsted to work there; however, I would remind you of what the prophet said to King David. There was a man who had only one little lamb. The king had guests come into town, and to serve them he took the little lamb, the one little lamb that the man had." (cf. 2 Sam. 12:3-4). He said, "I'd like you to read that, so you know the cost that I see it is for our diocese." So, he was really honest, but he had a sense of humor.

102. Cristofer: *Okay. So, this was what year again?*

103. Bishop Olmsted: This was 1979.

104. Cristofer: *So, in 1979, you were about to finish your doctorate, and you took on this role with what title?*

105. Bishop Olmsted: It was called an "adetto" of the Secretary of State; an attaché would be the word in French. Primarily, I helped with all of the correspondence, all the letters the pope needed to respond to, and helped with the translations of documents into English for all of the talks he would be giving in his travels around the world. There were the audience talks which had to be translated, telephone calls and other things that would come in English. At all the audiences, there would be one of us from the Segione Inglese, the English Section of the Secretary of State, who would be there with him. They would introduce all the English-speaking pilgrims who were there and explain to them that the Holy Father would be giving a blessing for the religious objects they brought, and he would be praying for those who were sick and their families.

106. So, it is the Secretary of State who assists the Holy Father in all of his personal needs, especially regarding his relations with the local churches around the world.

107. **Cristofer:** *So, you became an assistant to the Secretary of State?*

108. **Bishop Olmsted:** Yes, it was a staff of about seven English speakers; these were priests from English-speaking countries.

109. **Cristofer:** *So, did you share the duties of translating the documents, or were you the primary translator?*

110. **Bishop Olmsted:** We shared that together.

111. **Cristofer:** *You shared it. So, you shared it with seven priests?*

112. **Bishop Olmsted:** No one was doing a single translation; you'd always have at least another person look it over carefully to be sure it was really good. In fact, we specialized in English used in Africa, Asia, England, Canada, and the United States because the spelling is quite different, and some words could not be used in some countries as in others. So, we constantly were checking one another to be sure we weren't using anything that would be embarrassing to the pope.

113. **Cristofer:** *So, the staff probably reflected that diversity?*

114. **Bishop Olmsted:** It did.

115. **Cristofer:** *Were you the only American?*

116. **Bishop Olmsted:** No. Cardinal Rigali was the head of the section at the time. I ended up being there for nine and a half years, so other Americans came during that time as well.

117. Cristofer: *So, you finished your doctorate, and you stayed there?*

118. Bishop Olmsted: Yes, I did the doctoral defense a year after I started working there.

119. Cristofer: *So, you stayed there, and this was your post?*

120. Bishop Olmsted: It was. The whole time I did that, however, I was asked if I would serve as Assistant Spiritual Director to the North American College. I lived there, and I was the only person working in the Vatican who lived at the North American College at that time, but they had a tradition of having one priest there who was working in the Vatican. That meant I was able to live in a house where there were seminarians being trained; I did spiritual direction for them and had Mass for them.

121. Cristofer: *In your Vatican service experience, what did you take away with you from serving St. John Paul II?*

122. Bishop Olmsted: Well, I was always impressed by him and his example of prayer; he had a really deep sense of the presence of the Lord in adoration that was very evident. But also [I was impressed by] his courageous preaching of the good news. He always wanted to be sure that he was preaching the tough truths, the ones that were being controversially opposed or at least questioned. He wanted to be sure he was proclaiming these things to support the bishops and priests around the world who were preaching the good news. That struck me as a really good pastoral method and certainly impacted me later on.

123. Cristofer: *Would you share a few more intimate views of St. John Paul II from your days at the Secretariat of State? Could you share glimpses the public did not see on the night he was shot as well as the forgiveness of the shooter, etc.?*

124. Bishop Olmsted: When St. John Paul II forgave the would-be assassin, Mehmet Ali Ağca, for trying to take his life, it was not an afterthought. It flowed from trust in God's mercy and a lifelong habit of forgiving. Not only did he forgive his assailant in the first brief message he was able to make from his hospital bed, but also, months later, he went to the man's prison cell and, speaking with him like a brother, again offered his forgiveness. St. John Paul II also asked some of those who assisted him to make hospital visits to the persons who had been wounded by the same bullets that had passed through his body.

125. By the time he reached the age of twenty, the future pope had lost all his closest relatives – his sister, brother, and both parents. What could have made him an angry or morose young man instead led him to compassion for children of broken families, orphans, and widows. He trusted Jesus' words (John 14:18): "I will not leave you orphans. I will come to you."

126. Cristofer: *Mother Teresa and Pope John Paul II met several times. Did you also have a chance to meet Mother Teresa? Having been blessed to be in the presence of those who would later be recognized as saints, are there any particular learnings or memories of interactions with them that have stuck with you and impacted your faith or leadership style?*

127. Bishop Olmsted: I had the privilege of meeting Mother Teresa on several occasions; the most notable was when I was given the task of translating for her when she was conducting financial matters on behalf of the Missionaries of Charity. What impressed me was her insistence that every penny of what was donated to her Religious Institute be used to assist the poorest of the poor. At the conclusion of our meeting, she took both my hands in hers and, looking me in the eye, said: "Father, please pray that I and my Sisters never lose our spirit of joy."

128. Cristofer: *So, you worked in these offices for the Secretary of State for nine and a half years. How did you transition out of that role?*

129. Bishop Olmsted: Well, my bishop came over to do an Ad Limina visit toward the end of the first five years. He came into the Secretary of State, and they said, "We want you to release him for another five years." He said no at first, and then they said, "You know, the longer someone works here, the more valuable they are because they know how everything works. We know the kind of work he can do, and it's really hard to find that right now. He's most valuable to us." So, he wrote a letter to them saying he released me for five years from the very hour that he was giving the permission. He was there in November. So, rather than [the term] being five more full years, it was like four years and some months and some hours. So again, he was saying he didn't think they should be doing this, but he wasn't going to say no.

130. Cristofer: *Very interesting. And did your duties change, or did you do another five years of the same?*

131. Bishop Olmsted: It was the same kind of work.

132. Cristofer: *What came after that?*

133. Bishop Olmsted: I came back to the Diocese of Lincoln. I was delighted to be coming back, and I felt I needed a change. I'd been in Rome for over 16 years. I asked if I could have a six-month sabbatical at a monastery. So, I spent six months at Conception Abbey in the farm country of northwest Missouri.

134. Cristofer: *Let's talk a little about your leadership roles. So, you went back to Lincoln after a six-month sabbatical. What was your first assignment?*

135. Bishop Olmsted: My first assignment was to be a pastor at St. Vincent de Paul Parish in Seward, Nebraska. I was there for four years. It was a wonderful experience to finally be a pastor. It was a rural area, so I loved that. I had five nursing homes and a hospital, so I did quite a bit of work with the elderly and sick. I just enjoyed being a pastor for that large rural area. Some other smaller towns were also there.

136. Cristofer: *So, you were the pastor of a parish once?*

137. Bishop Olmsted: Once.

138. Cristofer: *Only once?*

139. Bishop Olmsted: Yes, only for four years.

140. Cristofer: *What did you get to do as a pastor that you never really got to do at any other time or place? What was unique about those years as a pastor?*

141. Bishop Olmsted: I would say two things had the biggest impact. One was working with the elderly because there were so many elderly people in all those institutions. I spent almost all of Wednesday going to all the nursing homes, having Mass in one and then Communion services in all the others. We had a hospital as well, so I was regularly supporting them.

142. The second was working with young people, especially those in high school. Only nine children coming for religious ed when I arrived, so I knew it was very inadequate. I put together a program for reaching teenagers through married couples who were really joyfully living their Faith. I wanted them [the children] to have a witness of a husband and wife who loved teenagers, who loved the Church, who loved Jesus, and who embraced all the Church's teaching. The only way that I felt the Church's teaching, like on *Humanae Vitae* (Paul VI 1968) and those things, would be acceptable is if the couples were living that. So, I chose [religious ed] teachers from among those that I got to know and was confident about. I also recruited natural family planning teachers from them. It was a chance to work with the education of young people and discern how the witness of lay couples would be so important, especially those [lay couples] who knew they were counter-cultural, but gratefully counter-cultural.

143. Cristofer: *It seems to me, through your formation, seminary, and serving St. John Paul II, you have decided that you need to be an ambassador of the Church's teaching on the Theology of the Body.*

144. Bishop Olmsted: Yes, very much so.

145. During my last year there [St. Vincent de Paul Parish in Seward, Nebraska], the Pontifical College Josephinum in Columbus, Ohio, through the Apostolic Nuncio, who was the prefect of that institution, asked that I be released to serve on its faculty.

146. Cristofer: *So, they knew you from Rome; they had heard of you?*

147. Bishop Olmsted: Yes.

148. Cristofer: *Okay, and what did your bishop say this time?*

149. Bishop Olmsted: Well, this was 1993, so I had a new bishop who came in 1992.

150. Cristofer: *What was his name?*

151. Bishop Olmsted: Bishop Fabian Bruskewitz, who had worked in the Vatican in the Congregation for Catholic Education. So, I knew him from there, but not really well. He was older than I, and he was an experienced servant of the Holy See. He gave permission for me to accept.

152. So, I went to the Pontifical College Josephinum, and I was there for six years. I began as Director of Personal Formation, and then I was named Rector and President of the Josephinum in my last three years.

153. Cristofer: *What happened after that? What was your next assignment?*

154. Bishop Olmsted: Next, I was assigned to be coadjutor bishop of Wichita, Kansas, in 1999.

155. Cristofer: *Is becoming a coadjutor bishop the same as an auxiliary bishop?*

156. Bishop Olmsted: No.

157. Cristofer: *What's the difference?*

158. Bishop Olmsted: A coadjutor bishop is someone who's appointed to assist the bishop and take over as soon as he retires or dies.

159. He [the Bishop of Wichita] had written and asked for a coadjutor bishop because his own health was somewhat fragile. He was in his late 60s; he wasn't near 75, so he asked for a coadjutor. I was appointed to assist him in that.

160. Cristofer: *What was your reaction when you learned that they wanted to make you a bishop?*

161. Bishop Olmsted: Well, I was shocked by it. One of the reasons I was shocked was because the nuncio didn't call me; I called him.

162. I called him because I was rector of the Josephinum, and every single faculty member had to be appointed by the Holy See through the nuncio. I had been waiting for months because we got a change of nuncio in January, and the new nuncio didn't arrive until February. That is when you have to especially recruit new faculty members. So, I had a whole list of people to be appointed. I had to explain all this to him [the new nuncio]. The former nuncio had left in December, and here it is, the middle of February. So, I called him up. I'd been trying to reach him. Finally, the nuncio took my call. I think it was Montalvo. [Apostolic Nuncio to the United States, Gabriel Montalvo Higuera, appointed December 7th, 1998.]

163. So, I said, "Your Excellency, this is Monsignor Olmsted from the Josephinum." And his first words were these, "Pope John Paul II has appointed you to be the coadjutor bishop of Wichita."

164. Cristofer: *But you were calling for a different reason!*

165. Bishop Olmsted: I've got these pages of questions and details of faculty members that have to be appointed and have to happen soon. That's all I'm thinking about.

166. Cristofer: *Oh, my goodness.*

167. Bishop Olmsted: And he said something totally unrelated, without a single introduction, nothing.

168. Cristofer: *Wow. Okay, so how did you respond?*

169. Bishop Olmsted: Well, first of all, I just said nothing. I was so stunned. And finally, he says, "Are you still there?" I said, "Yes, Your Excellency, but I didn't anticipate anything like this." And he said, "Well, do you say yes?" And I said, "Well, could I have 24 hours? I'm just totally shocked. I would like to have 24 hours to pray about this." So, he said, "Okay." But he said, "I think you should see this primarily as an act of obedience." That was a helpful thing to say.

170. So, when I went to prayer, I asked, "Is there some reason that I shouldn't and say no?" I tried to think, was there something in my life that was scandalous, or some reason it just wouldn't be good for the Church? So, it was out of that [prayer] that I said, "Well, I'll say yes." But this is really what I discerned; I couldn't think of any reason that I should say no if it is seen like an act of obedience because I've always been obedient.

171. Cristofer: *Okay! So, you became coadjutor bishop of the Diocese of Wichita. And how long before you became the bishop?*

172. Bishop Olmsted: About two and a half years. I was there for four and a half years, all told, but I was only two years as the ordinary of the diocese.

173. Cristofer: *And then they call you from Phoenix... or what happened?*

174. Bishop Olmsted: Well, there was a big crisis in the Diocese of Phoenix. Bishop O'Brien had resigned, and Archbishop Sheehan of Santa Fe was here as an administrator for six months. They needed someone as soon as possible, and they asked me to come. So, when the nuncio called me that time, I said yes. I was already a bishop, but I really knew nothing about the diocese. I had read of there being some problems here, but I just said yes and began to pray and think about coming to take over.

175. Cristofer: *Was this a different nuncio by this time, or was this the same nuncio that asked you to go to Wichita?*

176. Bishop Olmsted: Yes, it would have been the same nuncio, I think.

177. Cristofer: *Okay, Bishop, so you came to Phoenix, and you were the bishop for how many years?*

178. Bishop Olmsted: From 2003 till 2022, 19 years.

179. Cristofer: *Do you remember your first impressions of arriving in Phoenix or coming into the community?*

180. Bishop Olmsted: Well, I remember meeting Bishop O'Brien, and his first words were, "This is a wonderful diocese." He had been through a lot. It was a very difficult time. He was waiting for the criminal trial on charges of leaving the scene of a fatal accident to take place. His words really struck me because he was very sincere. He was really grateful to have served here. And I would agree with those words ["This is a wonderful diocese."].

181. My attention for the first six months had to be largely on just trying to get some momentum to move in a different direction because the front page of the paper every day was about the bishop being on trial. And then they also talked about the sexual abuse in the Church and the contentions that he had not handled that correctly.

182. Cristofer: *What immediately struck you as very distinct for the Diocese of Phoenix compared to the Diocese of Wichita?*

183. Bishop Olmsted: The Diocese of Phoenix was much bigger, and there was much more use of Spanish. There was a great need to be out present with the people, just to give them a sense that Christ is with us. I remember I was asked, "What's your vision for the Church?" and I said, "The vision I have for the Church isn't mine. It's the one that St. John Paul II gave. It's called *Ecclesia in America – the Encounter with the Living Jesus Christ* who leads us on this road of conversion, communion and solidarity. And that's what I will strive to do, to live that, and to help people encounter the Lord Jesus and to take up this path."

184. Cristofer: *As you were carrying out that vision of Ecclesia in America, what were the top priorities for you?*

185. Bishop Olmsted: Well, primarily, I would say the key thing was the very title, *Encounter with the Living Jesus Christ.* That was absolutely crucial. The bishop is supposed to represent Jesus. He's the high priest in the fullness of the priesthood. So, I felt that being with them, alongside the priests, was important and not always seen by myself. Jesus sent them out by two (Mark 6:7), so I saw myself as one with the pastor in every parish I was in. That was the two that were there, the pastor and the bishop as their pastor of the larger Church.

186. From the very beginning, I felt I needed never to rush through anything in a parish. St. Turibius was the first bishop ever canonized for all the New World, and that was his point. He had so much of South America, but he always said, "I never rush. I stay in that one parish for as long as it's needed before I go to the next one." That made a lot of sense to me. After ceremonies, lots of people wanted to say hello. I felt it was important to do that and to try to prepare homilies that were helpful for them.

187. Cristofer: *This was St. Turibius, Santo Toribio?*

188. Bishop Olmsted: Santo Toribio de Mogrovejo.

189. Cristofer: *Yes, another one of the three Dominican Peruvian saints. He was Spanish, I think?*

190. Bishop Olmsted: He was from Spain. He was a layman. He was a very capable canon lawyer and civil lawyer, whom the king and the pope strongly pressured to give up being a lay person to become a bishop. He [Santo Toribio] did not want to do that at all, but he was a great choice!

191. He's the one that gave Confirmation to St. Martin de Porres, and St. Rose of Lima.

192. Cristofer: *Interesting. Thank you! Okay, so you served the Diocese of Phoenix for 19 years. Now you're retired. What are the highlights, the most memorable parts, and some of the challenges? Tell me a little bit about that, looking back.*

193. Bishop Olmsted: Well, a bishop has to work well with his priests. That's who the people know best. They know their own pastor better than they know the bishop. So, I needed to work very closely with each priest, and try to develop a relationship with him that's both father and brother as far as possible. That depends on the age of priest somewhat and temperament. So that [establishing of relationships] would be memorable.

194. I was deeply impacted by St. John Paul II about the role of the laity. He was convinced that from his experience under communism and Nazism, in all of the situations of totalitarian government, the witness that would be most convincing was from lay people. So, he had to convince them of that. The fact that he kept constantly close to the university people, intellectuals, was because the communists really aimed to get the intellectuals on the side of the socialist regime. Also, the workers. He would go down and have Mass at least once a year, if not twice, with the miners down in the southern part. And artists. So, the role of the lay people was highly important for him. I saw that as pope, he would take special time for various groups of lay people.

195. Cristofer: *How did you try to emulate that special time for lay people yourself?*

196. Bishop Olmsted: Well, when I got to Wichita, one of the first things I did was to get to know the Catholic doctors and nurses who were there and to strengthen that community. I began to see that that made a difference. Doctors would give up prescribing contraception and come over because they weren't alone. They really found strength in the other doctors who were doing the same.

197. I helped start the first Legatus there [in Wichita], which is especially for executives. I had learned about that from St. John Paul II because he's the one who gave approval to Tom Monaghan. Then I also spent time with the Thomas More Society, with lawyers. Thomas More is my patron saint, and I really felt that there was a great need for lawyers to support each other in the Faith. I worked closely with the tribunal to get the tribunal's canon lawyers to know the civil lawyers that were there so that the profession would be built up in that way.

198. Cristofer: *So that was both in Wichita and Phoenix?*

199. Bishop Olmsted: It was, yes. I wasn't there [in Wichita] long enough to have a lot of time in that, but I really did see great progress in terms of the university people and the medical community there. So, when I came here [to Phoenix], that's what I picked up on as well. Within a month, I called Dr. Marci Moffitt. I don't know if you know Dr. Moffitt, but she's bilingual. She's just so heroic, really. I heard she had already stood up to Planned Parenthood and some others at a great cost to herself. I just wanted to get to know her, and through her, I got to know a lot of the other doctors. Then, we could build the Catholic Medical Association here through that. So even until this last year, she's always organized for Catholic medical students to meet their bishop at her home. She'd invite those medical students who were Catholic to come over, and I would have a good chance to meet them. It became very evident that if you can reach them before they're a doctor, before they start prescribing things that are contrary to their Faith, it'll make a huge difference.

200. Cristofer: *In their formative years.*

201. Bishop Olmsted: Exactly. Once they start doing things that are illicit and immoral, it's very hard for them to give it up. Very, very hard.

202. Cristofer: *I am getting the sense that you identified a key aspect of pastoring and shepherding the diocese by reaching out to specific communities of professionals.*

203. Bishop Olmsted: Exactly. That was my thought because I'd seen St. John Paul II do it. I knew about what he had done in that regard even before he was pope and how it really undercut the communist efforts to get these groups to be disenfranchised with the Church. It became the other way around. He was still a professor at the Catholic University of Lublin when he was chosen pope. Even as an archbishop, he kept teaching so he would have contact with those professionals.

204. Cristofer: *That's very interesting. Saint Josemaria Escriva, with whom I have a good friendship [strong devotion], used to say that the intellectuals were like the snow at the top of a mountain. When summer comes, the snow melts, and the water flows through all of the valleys. It describes the way in which the intellectuals can positively or negatively influence society. What are your thoughts on that?*

205. Bishop Olmsted: Well, I think that those given the grace of a profession that takes a lot of education to prepare for - and a lot of responsibilities come with it - I think it takes real courage for them to really live their Faith today in our highly secularized society. If they're doing that, they deserve the support of priests and bishops, and their appreciation as well. As we get to know them, we can help them see how their peers, especially the young ones coming into their profession, really need them. When they understand that themselves, they become real apostles. It's been so beautiful to see that happen.

206. Cristofer: *Could you tell me about some of the fruit you saw or that you are seeing from these efforts?*

207. Bishop Olmsted: One thing I've seen is the Catholic Medical Association; Dr. Moffitt was elected as chair of the Catholic Medical Association in the United States and Canada, and we hosted an international meeting here [in Phoenix]. Through her, we started the first-ever summer camp [Summer Scrubs] for young medical students. So, it shows what an impact one woman with such courage can have [on students] and among her peers as well.

208. Cristofer: *Thank you, Bishop! You have seen the importance of the family as someone who grew up in a Catholic family, then as a pastor, as a bishop and in so many different capacities; you have read about it in books and seen it firsthand. Please tell me about the importance of the family in terms of how you see it as informed by the Church [teachings and tradition] and how you brought that [insight] into practice as the Bishop of Phoenix.*

209. Bishop Olmsted: Well, God gave me by His providence some coincidences that are more than that. I think they were God's providence. Within the first weeks of starting to work with St. John Paul II, he started the General Audience talks on the Theology of the Body. Most of the time, with the General Audience talks, it was my duty to read them in Italian and write a summary that was about one-third as long in English. After giving the longer talk in Italian, he would read a summary in French, English, German, Spanish, and Polish. I ended up doing a lot of those; I had to understand fairly well what it said in Italian so I could write a summary of it in English. That was a great privilege, really.

210. It was difficult in the beginning because I didn't know where it was all going. We didn't get an outline of the whole thing. We just

got that one section of six or seven typed-out pages. But I knew he [St. John Paul II] was onto something there. Towards the end of those General Audiences, he talked about the reason he had done this. He didn't tell us earlier on, but only in the latter part because he was convinced that *Humanae Vitae* (Paul VI 1968) was true and that it was a vital, very key prophetic document. But it didn't sound like good news. It sounded like true news.

211. If it doesn't sound good, it's hard for the heart to grasp it when there's a real cost to doing so. So that's what he [St. John Paul II] tried to present with the Theology of the Body. That made a lot of sense to me. It showed me that if that is true, then we have to do everything we can to support family life. And we have to do it in a way that's as attractive as possible, rooted in truth, goodness and beauty.

212. Cristofer: *That, of course, was a staple of your time as Bishop of Phoenix. If you could, please describe initiatives you promoted on behalf of the family as bishop.*

213. Bishop Olmsted: One thing I should say is that my mother was one of the first people to be trained in natural family planning as a teacher through Dr. Hilger's natural procreative technology [NaPro Technology].

214. Cristofer: *When was that? Were you already a priest?*

215. Bishop Olmsted: I was. It was in the early 1980s, just shortly after I started working with St. John Paul II. She was asked to teach natural family planning because she had been trained as a nurse. She went up to Omaha and got her training from Dr. Hilgers. So, I had her witness.

216. I knew when she started teaching, there was only one priest who supported her in two counties in northern Kansas - no [other] priests, doctors, or nurses supported it. But within five years, a number of priests came to see her because these couples would go back and say, "Father, why don't you ever talk about natural family planning? We've been living it for the last couple of years. It's been a blessing for us." I learned from her, practically, what a difference it makes.

217. So, within months of when I became a pastor for the first time [St. Vincent de Paul Parish, Seward, Nebraska], I sent off couples [for training]. I interviewed four couples I thought could perhaps be trained in Omaha and then come back to help that parish. I saw what a difference that made. That was really, really helpful.

218. Coming here [to Phoenix], I found out we had natural family planning already being taught, but they [the groups] always need encouragement. I did everything I could to encourage them. Working with the Catholic Medical Association can really help. One group can help the other group; married couples can be helped by those who are in that [medical] profession.

219. **Cristofer:** *Sister Lucia, one of the three visionaries visited by Our Lady at Fatima, told us the family is under attack. Why is the family under attack?* (CNA Staff 2021)

220. **Bishop Olmsted:** Well, it seems to me that it's very significant in the Theology of the Body that you see the Blessed Trinity in some way is better understood by the symbolism of the love of husband, wife, and child. There's something of the mystery of the Blessed Trinity that a couple bears witness to, especially the image of the total gift of self. The fact that the priest says, this is my body, this is my blood, [similarly], in a certain way, a husband and wife, they're saying, I give my total self to you. There is an understanding that it's costly; it's a real share in the cross itself. It makes so much sense, connected with Church teaching and with the nature of the sacrifice involved in living a vocation.

221. **Cristofer:** *I try to stay in touch with the news and the different things happening in culture and in the Church. I try to see how it's all connected. It doesn't discourage me, but there's enough that a lot of people do get discouraged about everything that's happened just in the past few decades. Is there hope?*

222. **Bishop Olmsted:** Yes, I think it's important to remember Jesus is the light of the world. "The light shines in the darkness, and the darkness has not overcome it." (John 1:5). It's good for us to remember that example and those words. In many ways, the darker things are, the more the light stands out apart from that. So, the witness of a couple that is really living their Faith, the joy of

embracing those sacrifices and loving one another and loving their children, it impacts a lot of people when it's really lived. So, there's great hope in it. You know, we plant seeds one at a time or two at a time. He sends them out in twos (Mark 6:7). So, we can get discouraged because the Lord nearly always works in small ways, but He's always bringing about something beautiful, and good, and true.

223. Cristofer: *Thank you. The new Bishop of Phoenix, Bishop John Dolan, has brought into the light something we were all already aware of, worried about and cared about. He has made it one of the top priorities of his service as bishop. I'm sure you sympathize with the need as well to address the growing problems we have with mental health.*

224. Bishop Olmsted: Yes.

225. Cristofer: *Please share with me a little bit of your thoughts regarding the direction that the bishop is taking on this issue. It seems to be graver and a lot more profound and complex than I thought it would be at first.*

226. Bishop Olmsted: I really think it's God's providence that he [Bishop Dolan] has been brought here. The very first night that I met him, the night before he was publicly introduced, I said, "Tell me a little bit about yourself." Two things struck me immediately. One, he said, "I come from a large Irish Catholic family, which has been a real blessing for me, but" he said, "It's a family that has suffered greatly because of suicide." So, I asked him to say a little more about that.

227. He [Bishop Dolan] had just finished writing a book on suicide together with a deacon. It really struck me that from his own life, he knows what people suffer when a loved one commits suicide or attempts to commit suicide, and how the whole family is impacted. Two weeks after he was here, another sibling committed suicide. His witness in that [experience], I think, is really important, vitally important. So, I think it's a blessing that he's so open about this.

228. I'm glad the Mass Bishop Dolan had at the Cathedral for those who have lost a loved one through suicide was received so openly with a sense that this is what the Holy Spirit wants us to do. I'm very

happy about that happening. Stress and mental illness seem to be growing because of COVID and other things happening in the breakdown of marriage and society.

229. Cristofer: *It's amazing how it all seems to be connected. Suicide is, of course, one of the most horrible outcomes that mental health problems can have, but also addictions, substance abuse, and homelessness are connected to it. There are so many different aspects of it. Have you seen the Universal Church touch on this issue enough? Will it be becoming more and more relevant? Is there still room for us as a Universal Church to address it?*

230. Bishop Olmsted: I think so. It seems to me that society itself is really suffering. There are tensions and things in society that may be linked with mental illness, and some within human beings themselves. But there's certainly no doubt that, as St. John Paul II said in St. Louis in 1999, "As the family goes, so goes the nation" (see also Homily 1986). And so, if the family is suffering from suicide and other mental health problems, then certainly the whole society is being impacted in a powerful way. For that reason, I think God is raising Bishop Dolan up in this diocese, and maybe even beyond this diocese, to be a light about this particular need for the Church - to be a witness of the light of Christ.

231. Cristofer: *In a world filled with so much sadness and sin, many younger professionals (and older ones, too!) are confused and concerned about the future. Please speak about how a person can turn from this sense of despair and confusion to peace and trust.*

232. Bishop Olmsted: Keep in mind the difference between happiness and pleasure. Happiness flows from living the Beatitudes and from accepting whatever "Crosses" God's providence places on our path. Discover the wisdom of Romans 12:15-16, "Rejoice with those who rejoice, weep with those who weep....do not be haughty but associate with the lowly; do not be wise in your own estimation."

233. Just as Jesus was a sign of contradiction in his day, be prepared for contradictions and misunderstandings when you faithfully follow Jesus. The Catholic writer Flannery O'Connor reportedly said, "The truth will make you odd!" Since Jesus is the Way and the Truth,

honesty always will make you odd, but if done for the love of Christ, it will also make you "awed."

234. Cristofer: *Thank you, Bishop! So, here are a few final questions to close the section on life. Why is life precious? And what is a life well lived for a Catholic?*

235. Bishop Olmsted: Well, life is precious because God is the source of life. Everything He made is good. After He created man and woman, He said it was very good (Gen. 1:31). So human life is very good. There is reflected within that the image of God himself as Trinity and His total gift of self. The Father giving the Son; the Father and the Son giving the Holy Spirit; Jesus' death on the cross, et cetera. There's something in that which is really, really powerful and needed. So, life, the witness to life, has so many layers. There are so many different ways we can witness to life - and that are needed for us to do so!

236. Cristofer: *The second part was, what is a life well lived for a Catholic? I'm thinking more of lay Catholics. How can they examine their life, whether they're beginning to live it or looking back at it and know that they lived life well?*

237. Bishop Olmsted: Right. Well, Jesus said, "I came that they might have life and have it more abundantly." (John 10:10). I think once we encounter Him and give our life to Him, we begin to discover there's a greater fullness to our life that's happening individually in our own soul. Then, with our relationships, there is a healing or a strengthening that takes place and that sense of the ability to live a life that's good and true and beautiful. The ability, not by our own strength at all, but by the mercy of God and the grace of God, to be faithful in relationships and to be reconciled when there's brokenness there. God can take broken things and make them even stronger. And He does and wants to do so!

238. The crucifix is always a sign of great hope for us. So, yes, there's a life that can be well lived, but not by my own kind of white-knuckling determination, but by my surrender of myself into God's hands because He will take and bring more and more life out of that.

---

239. Cristofer: *What would you attribute as the single most important thing in your life?*

240. Bishop Olmsted: Stay firmly on the path that puts Jesus first in your life and facilitates your keeping Him first. Keep the eyes of your heart fixed on Jesus (cf. Heb. 12:2). Set aside time at the beginning and the conclusion of each day to be with Him. Be sure that one of these times lasts at least fifteen minutes. Daily prayer, alone and with others, keeps us anchored in Christ.

Life

Faith

Leadership

Part 2
Faith

Jesus didn't come to make life easier for us. He came to make life better (John 10:10). He came to lead us to something that's good and true and beautiful, but which costs greatly. (para. 248)

Jesus promised, "...if two of you agree on earth about anything for which they are to pray, it shall be granted to them by my heavenly Father" (Matt. 18:19). The Lord is true to His promise. (para. 325)

---

241. Cristofer: *It seems to me you've always had a pretty strong faith. You were certain, very certain, about your vocation from an early age. Did you ever have any doubts at all about your faith, or has there ever been a dark night? Anything like that?*

242. Bishop Olmsted: There's never been a time when I really had great temptations against faith and trust in Christ. Certainly, the longer I live, the more I'm aware of my own weaknesses. And certainly, I know that it's only by the mercy of God that each day, I'm able to strive to be faithful to Him.

243. From the time I started to live the sacramental life of the Church, my family went to Confession every two weeks. I've followed that pattern ever since, which has been very helpful in my life. I would say that my faith is heavily nourished by the mercy of God in the Sacrament of Penance, which I see as a really great gift for the Church - often not appreciated as much as needed in the present Church.

244. And then, the Eucharist itself, both in terms of celebration of the Eucharist as a priest and also in terms of adoration, just spending time with Jesus alone in the Eucharist. Those have been great, great blessings for me and have really helped keep my faith alive. So, there's not been a major crisis in that regard.

245. Cristofer: *Is the Catholic Faith difficult? What would you say to those who describe it as a rigid set of rules?*

246. Bishop Olmsted: I would say that it's an encounter with the Lord Jesus Christ. It's the opposite of rules. It's really living in a relationship of love and experiencing being chosen. [Jesus said,] "It was not you who choose me, but I who chose you" (John 15:16). That's really true. He didn't choose us because we're worthy, and He didn't choose us because there's anything in us that's better than anyone else at all. Caryll Houselander talks about the loveliest hour and loving the least. (Houselander 1944) That makes a lot of sense to me. He [the Lord] is always seeking out the lost and the one who feels they're too small to be noticed. I think our faith is impacted by our awareness that God's love is so much greater, and His mercy is so much greater than we could ever imagine - and it's always there.

247. Cristofer: *Thank you, Bishop. You've answered in terms of faith being what it is in its essence, which is a relationship with Christ. But in terms of the actual practice of the Faith, I think it is perhaps less than that. At least for the laity, it is less of that robust, rigorous program of spiritual growth and development than it once was. So, do you agree, in a sense, that perhaps we're not asking enough of the laity? Wherever I turn, there seem to be exceptions granted to the laity, extraordinary things taking place. Why is there such a need for all of this accommodation? My concern would be that we're not being boldly Catholic.*

248. Bishop Olmsted: Yes, I certainly see the tendencies in various parts of the Body of Christ, the Church, which don't realize that unless you take up your cross each day, you cannot be my [Jesus'] disciple (cf. Luke 9:23). Jesus didn't come to make life easier for us. He came to make life better (John 10:10). He came to lead us to something that's good and true and beautiful, but which costs greatly.

249. So, it's not helpful to make it look as if there's not a big cost to this. I think we always need to appreciate and witness to the fact that great blessings come from being faithful, but it would not be helpful to make it look as if that's easy to do. It would be very unhelpful, in fact. Jesus never did that. He was always talking about it. "Whoever wishes to come after me must deny himself, take up his cross, and

follow me" (Matt. 16:24). He was very concretely putting things before the apostles that would cost them greatly themselves.

250. That's why I think we need to realize that, as the *Catechism* says, prayer is a battle (CCC 2573, 2725), and the Christian life is a battle (CCC 409) (The Holy See 2019). It's a constant battle because the evil one is certainly at work; we have to anticipate and expect that will be the case. On the other hand, he [the devil] is just a fallen angel, and he's no stronger than the good angels. He certainly is nothing compared to the power of Divine Mercy.

251. So, both of those [cross and battle] we have to be aware of, but it would not be helpful if we tried to water things down. It's the opposite. I think we need to lift up what's possible with God's grace - not our strength - but God's grace (CCC 2805). We should strive to take up those challenges that the Lord gives us.

252. Cristofer: *I observe that there is a lot of confusion in the laity as to what exactly the character of their lay vocation is. What would you say are the distinctive marks of living the Faith according to the lay vocation as opposed to the religious consecrated vocation?*

253. Bishop Olmsted: I think one would be [in terms of] ordinary and another one would be [in terms of] profession. Ordinary - it's in the ordinary circumstances of everyday life where the quality of our life is impacted as we try just to live throughout each day with a real sense of gratitude to God and embracing whatever challenges and duties the Lord is giving us that day. It is in the ordinary things that [understanding vocation] happens. It's in the ordinary life of a marriage, within a home, of being a mother, of being a father, of being a colleague, of being a friend; it is in those relationships.

254. But then there is profession, too; there's a need for us to realize that professions themselves have a long history and culture. [For example], the medical profession and the legal profession go way back, and without them, society would suffer greatly. When you get confusion about leadership in those areas, great suffering will come about because of that. So, we need to appreciate the fact that if God calls you to a profession, there are a lot of duties that come with that – opportunities - but duties as well. There will be moments when it will require real courage to stand up within that [profession] for a

truth that somehow is being obfuscated and forgotten but needs to be clearly articulated, supported and explained.

255. Cristofer: *So, professions need to be accepted as vocations within the lay vocation?*

256. Bishop Olmsted: Yes, exactly. Calls within a call. Mother Teresa talked about that herself. She was called to be a religious sister, but then she was called to found a new religious community -coming out from within what she had [originally] been a part of. I think that's true for lay people too.

257. Cristofer: *Let's talk a little bit about the Second Vatican Council. In simple terms, what was the council and was it successful? Did it accomplish what it set out to do?*

258. Bishop Olmsted: First of all, I think it's important to remember that from the beginning, a signature part of the council was *Lumen Gentium,* the dogmatic constitution on the nature of the Church (Second Vatican Council 1964). That's in the title, *Lumen Gentium*, a light to the peoples, a light to the nations. So obviously, Jesus is the light to the nations, but His body, His mystical body, His Church - it's through that He shows His light to the world. That's the primary reason that the council was called less than 20 years after WWII. The War was a great darkness - to see so much horrible suffering and that ongoing totalitarian governments have no recognition of the value of human life and some basic principles that have guided us down through history.

259. Lumen Gentium itself is a really major document, and within it, it has one whole section on the role of the laity, which is very significant. It was an emphasis that we didn't see in many Church documents before that, partly because education and the Industrial Revolution had happened within a hundred years before that council. So those made possible an awareness of participation of far more people in the professions. So that document, I think, is really a very important document. There's so much more within it that still needs to be embraced and really lived out.

260. Now, parts of it are in other places, such as a document on the role of the laity, the *Apostolicam Actuositatem.* (Second Vatican

Council 1965) That document certainly builds from *Lumen Gentium* and articulates even more broadly. So that's also a really important document. Another very important document is *Dei Verbum*, which is on the Church's understanding of divine revelation (Second Vatican Council 1965). Our God is a God who speaks, and He is constantly speaking to us. He's calling out to us. He's inviting us through the power of His word. There's so much more yet to be mined, brought forward, and lived that's there.

261. The *Sacrosanctum Concilium* (Second Vatican Council 1963), which is the one on the divine liturgy, I would say wasn't strategically released, [coming] before *Lumen Gentium*. Looking back, it may have put us in a position of not even having the context of the mystery of the Church within which to see why you would have some kind of adaptation of the Sacred Liturgy. So, the first major document released by the Second Vatican Council was on the liturgy. But so many people, because it wasn't explained in depth and with the full catechesis needed, just saw it as change for change's sake rather than an invitation, a call, to enter into the great paschal mystery of Jesus Christ that the liturgy is meant to present to us. I think we're just beginning to do that [catechesis]. I think the implementation of [changes to] the liturgical life of the Church was a bumpy road, and there are still things that we're suffering from because of that.

262. **Cristofer:** *That was going to be my next question. Earlier, you talked about the turmoil that occurred in the years after the Second Vatican Council. When lay Catholics or even clergy speak about the Second Vatican Council today, they often tend to focus on the changes in the liturgy and then on the ecumenical aspects of the council. Unfortunately, many Catholics will argue about this all day long, and there's much to be discussed, but I feel that we completely neglect to touch on the bold, urgent challenge that the council had for the laity. It's like the other two topics overpower the third one, and it gets completely dismissed.*

263. *So please tell me a little bit about the importance of the fact that the council defined what the lay vocation was to a laity that for so many years thought that we didn't have a path to sanctity; maybe the most we could hope for was purgatory, and that holiness wasn't for*

everybody. Maybe the church never said it, and maybe that was a misunderstanding before the council.

264. The council, I think, was very clear in terms of who the laity are and our vocation; it gave us our marching orders. But all of that seems to remain neglected, lost in the shuffle of the discussion on the liturgy and ecumenical aspects of the council.

265. Bishop Olmsted: I agree the role of the laity was very much one of the major things they [the Council] wanted us to see in *Lumen Gentium*. That's why they even added a second document on the active role of the laity. So, I agree that's very much the case. I also think that the inadequate and only partial implementation of the document on the Sacred Liturgy contributed to that confusion; many lay people felt what Vatican II made possible was that I could be a reader. This is really my lay vocation. No, your lay vocation is primarily as a lay person and not within the liturgy. That's where you go to celebrate the great paschal mystery and are enriched by that, but your primary role is within your family and within your profession.

266. I think there was so much of a thing about recruiting people to be readers and all, that lay people began to think that was the [vocation of] the lay people; that's what the Church wanted the lay people to be doing. We welcome some people to help give out Communion and be readers. [However,] we above all want them to be living that Faith and explaining that Faith within their home, and with their colleagues and with lay people in society. So, I think a poor implementation of *Sacrosanctum Concilium* impacted a poor understanding of the lay role in the Church.

267. Cristofer: *Thank you. We've talked about the unfortunate turbulence in the outcomes of the council, but are there some good outcomes of the council that you are pleased to see?*

268. Bishop Olmsted: I'm pleased Catholics are more and more aware of how important the Word of God is for our life in Christ. I think maybe 15 percent of the Bible was found in the Lectionary of the Mass before the revisions, and now, with the three-year cycle of Sunday readings and a two-year cycle of Daily Mass readings, we must use at least 85 percent of the Bible. That's a great difference.

Now, that's just looking at it quantitatively, you might say, but it says something about the Church really wanting to feed us day by day with the Word of God.

269. That's not a small thing at all because there's such a great need for us to believe that God desires to speak to us. He does speak to us and teach us. His truth sets us free. That truth is a person more than a thing (CCC 1039). There's just so much richness in that. I think that could really impact lay people's understanding of themselves and where they find rich food and rich drink for living their life in Christ (CCC 1407-1408).

270. Cristofer: *Bishop, there is a litany of things that are threats to the Catholic Church right now; the Church is fighting so many battles. What would you say is the single most dangerous threat to the Faith today?*

271. Bishop Olmsted: Well, certainly, one of them has to be a failure to tell the truth. To be witnesses to the truth and to believe the truth sets us free, is really a major thing. Jesus calls the devil "the father of lies" (John 8:44), so whenever we are not facing the truth squarely, that's a real, real danger. Rather than freedom, there's binding and being enslaved in that, so that's a really big one.

272. A second one that's a prominent problem right now is the opposite of "Blessed are the clean of heart, for they will see God" (Matt. 5:8). We need to remember that great blessing, but there are so many things in our society which are impure, which are pornographic, and which are twisting the image of the human person made in the image of God.

273. So, I would see both of those as very concrete [threats] and sadly doing great, great harm. The Church has a role [to help address] that for certain. It has the means because of the sacraments that are there. There's a role for every member of the Church, lay people, as well as those who are ordained or those who are in religious life; we all have a role to play in that [witnessing to the truth and being clean of heart].

274. Cristofer: *An uncomfortable topic to talk about, and for me to ask about, but something we can't ignore, is the series of sex abuse* *scandals in the Church. There's a wound in the Church; it has caused so much damage, so much pain, so much hurt. What do the lay people do when we see this? Many of us are practicing and continue to be faithful and have not abandoned the Faith, but it's a great discouragement and disappointment. It's a minority within the clergy that took part in these scandals that continue to come to light, but what is the laity to make of this? It's historical; it's just so many years that this has taken place. When a lay person looks at his or her Church and looks at this big stain, this big wound, what are we to make of it?*

275. Bishop Olmsted: It's a very good question, and there are various dimensions to it. I think, first of all, we grieve because there has been terrible abuse that was inflicted by those who were called to be servant ministers of others. That's a great scandal, and scandal always causes grave damage. We're supposed to be witnesses of Christ, convincing witnesses of Christ, and this is the exact opposite. So, we have to grieve; we have to acknowledge it. We have to ask forgiveness as a Church. As a bishop representing the Church, I was required to do that often, and I tried to do it frequently with those who had been abused. I met with many victims throughout my time as a bishop, going back to my time in Wichita.

276. I think we have to start with the fact that Jesus came to call sinners and that, certainly, when we sin, we really do grave harm. It always poisons; it always damages; it always discourages. Crisis can make us stronger, but there's grave, grave damage that comes from this. So, I think we need to start with that.

277. Cristofer: *Are these the most difficult times the Church has lived, or not? What other times in the history of the Church would you say have been as grave or as challenging?*

278. Bishop Olmsted: Well, I think this is a real true scandal. Not only did priests and others seriously break with their great responsibility to be a trusted father figure - that's huge, huge - but also that it was not dealt with decisively by bishops or religious superiors. The fact that they even covered it up is a huge scandal. It's a scandal on top of the scandal, and it shows unhealthy self-protection rather than really caring about the most vulnerable and harmed person in the Church. So that's why I think we really need to weep with those who weep (Rom. 12:15), and we need to face this disaster very squarely and publicly right now. If we cannot do that, we will be held accountable, and we should be held accountable.

279. The fact that we've had betrayal and scandal - Judas is already there, one of the twelve. Then, you have all the mistakes of the others, [the other apostles], which are pointed out. So, we can [see how to] deal with sinfulness, especially when we bring it to Christ.

280. People bring it there [to Christ], but if we're part of covering it up and not facing it squarely, and especially holding accountable those who should be trustworthy, there's no way we can recover until we do that very, very honestly. I think if we do that, at some point, because we all deal with sin, that's the healing needed in all these different things. We certainly have many broken marriages, which cause huge harm to children. God could use it [the example of accountability, mercy and forgiveness] in a way there. But we need to attend, right now, to what is our duty in the present moment.

281. Cristofer: *While never perfect, most recognize a period in history or civilization that Christians nostalgically refer to as Christendom. Is there hope to bring Christendom back? Should we even be thinking in those terms, and what would it take to accomplish it?*

282. Bishop Olmsted: First of all, God is the author of history. We have to respond to Him in history at this present time, and we're so far away from Christendom. However, there are people who don't know or don't believe that and who long for what, if it were to happen, would take a great time to happen. We have to be about where we are right now. We have to live in the reality of the present moment that's here. We can learn from the good things from the past, but we can't nostalgically try to live in that when that's not the reality now.

283. Cristofer: *Focus on the present - but should we be aiming, and can we draw inspiration [from Christendom], or should we just move on?*

284. Bishop Olmsted: I think we should draw inspiration from the Church of the first three centuries, which is where you had the whole society and the culture that was opposite, completely opposite, of the good news of Jesus Christ. The Church never grew more quickly than at that time, and the witness was incredibly strong because it was the opposite of what was there [in society]. The light was shining in the face of great darkness (John 1:5), and so many people wanted to be part of this because it was heroic; it was true. So, I think the better model is the model of the courageous evangelization of the first three centuries.

285. Cristofer: *The early Christians?*

286. Bishop Olmsted: Yes, because we're seeing that the popular culture is very anti-Christian, and that's what they were [also] facing then. They were gladly doing that [witnessing] because they knew that their message would be a sign of contradiction. The world needed to see that we don't agree and it's not helpful for anybody in the world to be imbibing that [popular culture], drinking it down and falling for its lies.

287. Cristofer: *Today, we live in a world that's plagued with ideologies. There's a list that continues to grow of new ideas, falsehoods, and lies. Which are the most problematic, or can you point out some of the ideologies and some of the things that are really harming humanity today?*

288. Bishop Olmsted: The devil is very clever when it comes to evil, so there are a lot of things that we're dealing with without a doubt. Which ones are the worst? I think it's a great danger when we move into what's the opposite of reality. Ideologies do that. They get us to think that something's real when it isn't real. Certainly, that would be [harmful] because it's linked with the lack of being rooted in truth and rightness. The greatest of these is love, so the opposite of that is whatever is not loving.

289. There's certainly a lot of division right now. There's a lot of anger. There's a great temptation to join the voices that are angry and resentful. The opposite of charity is really widespread. And the media, I think, finds a way to get itself supported financially often by making people even more angry, so there are many temptations to do that. Also, people can feel self-righteously angry, and that's a great danger. We should be angry at what's wrong. But, we have to be very

careful when we do that we don't overstep as if we're better than others and not contributing some as well by our own sinfulness.

290. Cristofer: *Thank you. Moving in a different direction, is there a distinctive mark to American Catholicism? What would you say are some of the unique contributions of the Catholic Church in the United States to the Universal Church? What are some values that we still have, or were at some point stronger, that we should hold on to?*

291. Bishop Olmsted: Your question makes me think of my very dear friend, Bishop Felipe Estevez. He was a Cuban refugee who came to this country when he was 14. He would right away start answering that America has some really important gifts that the world needs. One of them that he often picks up on is creativity. We've gone to [a theme park] together a couple of times. He said, "This is creativity. America constantly does this. It creatively does things with the use of the imagination that can actually help us appreciate the genius of human beings and enjoy being together." That would be one thing he would say. I think sometimes when you've come from another country - you and I have both lived in other countries - there is something about being able to see [the culture] in a way that the people [living] there, absorbed in it, don't notice what's there.

292. There's something about creativity that's true for Americans, but I don't know if we're as creative now or as ready to be creative as we once were. I think being creative is a great thing because we're made in the image of a Creator - a Father and a Creator. I would like to think that is something we still strive for. Those in the Church who are really living their Faith are often creative because the Lord gives us creative gifts to overcome evil.

293. Cristofer: *In addition to the Bible and books on saints that you already mentioned, can you tell us about other books and authors that you have found particularly impactful for the development of your faith and leadership?*

294. Bishop Olmsted: For more than fifty years, I have loved the writings of [American authors] Dorothy Day, especially *The Long Loneliness* (1952) and *Loaves and Fishes* (1963), and Flannery O'Connor's short stories and the collections of her letters: *The Habit of Being* (1979). Sherry Boas is a terrific storyteller, especially *Until*

Lily (2011) and *Laughter of Angels* (2019) and the poetry of Jessica Powers [a Carmelite Nun] I return to often (1999). One of my favorite [Canadian] novelists is Michael D. O'Brien, especially *Island of the World* (2010) and *The Father's Tale* (2011)

295. The writings of Father Jacques Philippe inspire me, especially *Priestly Fatherhood* (2021). I have a special devotion to St. Catherine of Siena and appreciate her *Dialogue* (1991), plus the collections of her "Letters" and "Prayers." Thomas More is my patron saint, and I have been greatly inspired by his heroic life, faithful witness to Christ, his letters, and books about him.

296. Cristofer: *What are some of your favorite movies or documentaries?*

297. Bishop Olmsted: *Sound of Freedom* (Caviezel 2023) and *The Quiet Girl* (Crowley 2022) are two movies that I have appreciated recently.

298. Cristofer: *When we teach at TLI, trends begin to emerge, and it's very clear, very evident, that whether we're talking about immigration, life, education, health - whatever topic we're talking about - it always goes back to the respect and the protection of the dignity of the human person. Why is that the case with Church teaching?*

299. Bishop Olmsted: The common good and the dignity of every human person are two principles the Catholic Church is always looking to. Whenever we're facing any problem, we often have to come back to those two things. How is this going to impact the common good and, especially, each individual person's human dignity?

300. It is true that we are made in the image of God. Our dignity comes from God. When the dignity of the human person is not acknowledged and when it's being twisted, that's a real sign that the evil one is at work there. At that time, we need to step into the breach and defend the dignity of that human person. We see it, sadly, in our society in every kind of sector, from the youngest, the unborn, to the oldest, to pornography's misuse of people. There are so many ways

that the human dignity of the person is being trampled upon at the present time, and sometimes [the trampling is] celebrated.

301. Cristofer: *Bishop, one of my favorite things the Church teaches is the redemptive value of suffering. I'd like you to address that a little bit because I feel there are so many Catholics who don't understand that, unlike the rest of the world, we can make something of suffering, which is an inescapable part of the human experience. Please tell me a little bit about how Catholics should approach suffering, which is something we are all going to go through.*

302. Bishop Olmsted: It's for very good reason that we begin our prayer with the sign of the cross, we end our prayer with the sign of the cross, we give a blessing with the sign of the cross, and we have images of the crucifix in so many places - on the rosary, in the churches, etc. [It is] because of the mystery of suffering; we were redeemed through the suffering and death of Jesus on the cross and His resurrection.

303. Keeping all that together is important because that whole paschal mystery, that whole passage, begins with the fact of self-emptying and the suffering that is there. Its value is reinforced by the risen Lord appearing with His wounds still in His body, but they're glorified wounds (John 20:27-29). Those glorified wounds remind us that the suffering is how He made the total gift of himself to the Father and how we ourselves, too, I mean all the way up to the moment of our own death, surrender back to the Father. It's within those wounds that Jesus will be present. That's why I think the liturgical language used throughout the Eucharistic Prayer frequently mentions the blood of Christ. It links us very much with that mystery of the suffering of Christ being the way that He redeems us, washes away our sins, and gives us new life in his Son.

304. Cristofer: *What would be a practical "to do"/laundry list for young professionals to prepare and keep themselves pure and strong to serve our Lord? For example, not just a list of spiritual exercises or prayers but very simple specific practices.*

305. Bishop Olmsted: Your job or profession is more than earning a living; it is where Jesus invites you to be His witness.

306. Be the best professional you can be and the best servant of the Gospel. Pray for your colleagues and build healthy relationships with them.

307. Take to heart the words of St. John Paul II (*Redemptor Hominis*),

> *Man cannot live without love. He remains ... incomprehensible [to] himself, his life is senseless, if love is not revealed to him, if he does not encounter love, if he does not experience it and make it his own, if he does not participate intimately in it.*

308. Do not be afraid to have conversations about substantial topics like love, faith, and life.

309. Remember Jesus' words, "Blessed are the clean of heart for they will see God" (Matt. 5:8). In a culture with twisted notions of gender, sexuality, and marriage, keep a close watch on your imagination and your use of screens. Cultivate the virtues of chastity, charity, and justice.

310. Trust the truth; avoid telling even 'little white lies.' There is a reason that Jesus calls the devil "the father of lies" (John 8:44). Jesus is the truth that sets us free. He also is the Love that calms restless hearts and, when surrendered to Him, ignites them with charity and mercy.

311. Put Jesus first in your life and adopt habits that keep Him first. If your heart is becoming lukewarm, examine your conscience as to why; beg Jesus for the grace of conversion. Beware of sins of omission; they easily corrupt the soul and provide fertile ground for indifference and mediocrity.

312. If you notice the fire of your faith diminishing, rekindle the fire through the Sacraments, in particular the Eucharist and Confession. A great antidote to hypocrisy is the regular reception of the Sacrament of Penance.

313. Imitate Jesus' habit of seeking to serve, not to be served. Never was He blind to the poor and forgotten. His first priority was the least ones of the Kingdom of God.

314. Each year, during Advent and Lent, ask yourself, "Am I putting the interests of others ahead of my own, including the interests of co-workers, colleagues, and family members?"

315. If married, be intentional about loving your spouse, taking time to build your domestic church, and to stand up for a culture of life. Healthy marriages and good friends build up Christ's Body, the Church.

316. Cristofer: *Can you talk about your personal experience of keeping Sunday as a day of rest, both before becoming a priest and then after?*

317. Bishop Olmsted: I grew up on a farm where Sunday was always a day of rest from the work of planting, cultivating, harvesting, and so forth. That example set by my parents formed in me a firm commitment to the commandment: Remember to keep holy the Lord's Day (cf. Exod. 20:8).

318. Not until I was sent as a young priest to do doctoral studies in Rome did I experience the need to put in place practices that would keep Sunday a day of rest, set apart from the other six days. The problem arose from the practice of many student priests working on their studies diligently during the week and then taking a break from their studies on Friday evenings and Saturdays. It was exacerbated by the custom of many professors scheduling exams and papers that were due on Mondays. As a result, student priests tended to work on their studies each Sunday.

319. Within a few months, I had the feeling that Sunday was no longer a day of rest for me. So, I made a resolution to work on Friday evenings and Saturdays but never again to do schoolwork on Sundays. In addition to Sunday Mass, I would visit museums, spend time with friends, make a day trip to holy places near Rome, and so forth. With that resolution, Sunday returned to being my favorite day of the week - and has remained so ever since.

320. Cristofer: *Can you tell us a little about some of the most memorable, maybe even miraculous, events you have firsthand knowledge of?*

321. Bishop Olmsted: Dafne Gutierrez, a wife and mother of three children, was blind. When relics of St. Sharbel were brought to St. Joseph Maronite Church in Phoenix for a period of three days, she attended several of the liturgies celebrated there in Spanish, Latin, Aramaic, Greek, and English. She venerated the relics and was anointed with the holy oil from Fr. Sharbel's tomb in Lebanon. Within only a day or two, her eyesight was completely restored.

322. I was one of several priests who celebrated Mass during those days and heard Confessions. After the miracle, when I met with Dafne, she verified that she had indeed been healed. A medical doctor also examined her and gave testimony that there was no medical or scientific explanation of the miracle (St. Joseph Maronite Catholic Church in Phoenix, Arizona 2016).

323. Paul Zucarelli's story is already well known through the books that he published (Zucarelli 2018). One key part of the miracle occurred when Paul's adult son, Michael, drove across town to St. Paul's Parish, where I had just celebrated Mass and I was at the exit of the church greeting people who had been present. As Michael came into the church, he noticed me greeting people after Mass.

324. His father's heart had stopped beating several times, and the physician had said there was no hope of survival. When that happened, Michael hurried to his car and drove to a church where he could find a priest; I was the first he found.

325. [Afterwards,] the physician said that there was no medical or scientific explanation for [Paul Zucarelli's] miracle. Jesus promised, "...if two of you agree on earth about anything for which they are to pray, it shall be granted to them by my heavenly Father" (Matt. 18:19). The Lord is true to His promise.

Holy Sacraments: Give me the Grace
St. Thomas More

Give me the grace
to long for
Your Holy Sacraments,
and especially to rejoice
in the presence of Your body,
sweet Savior Christ,
in the Holy Sacrament of the altar.
Amen.

SUGGESTED PRAYER
From a favorite saint

The Prayer of Abandonment
St. Charles de Foucauld

Father,
I abandon myself
into your hands;
do with me what you will.
Whatever you may do, I thank you:
I am ready for all, I accept all.
Let only your will be done in me,
and in all your creatures.
I wish no more than this, O Lord.

Into your hands
I commend my soul;
I offer it to you
with all the love of my heart,
for I love you, Lord,
and so need to give myself,
to surrender myself
into your hands,
without reserve,
and with boundless confidence,
for you are my Father.

Part 3
Leadership

There's something in being witnesses to the truth, especially to the truth which is Jesus himself. That is a vital part of leadership because those words [go, teach] are not only for the apostles; they are for every member of the Church. I would put that at the heart of leadership. (para. 372) (cf. Matt. 28:19-20)

So that call to holiness, the willingness to listen, to take it in and to be really convinced about it, and joyful that I have been called to do this - those are great blessings that the world needs. Lay people's witness is vitally needed for others to trust in that call. (para. 391)

---

326. Cristofer: *How much of priesthood is leadership? Is priesthood simply all leadership? There are so many dimensions to being a priest. How much of being a priest is being a leader?*

327. Bishop Olmsted: That's a good question. Being a priest conforms us more to Jesus as the head of the Church, the Redeemer, the Savior and Lord. So, if He's the head of the Church, then there is leadership that He wishes to exercise through very, very weak human beings, but He wishes and has bound himself to doing it in that way.

328. So, [priestly] leadership needs always to be linked with Jesus as the head of the Church. If we are to do that and be an image of that, then He will give us the grace and, therefore, the responsibility to lead. So, it has to be part of a priesthood. It could not be otherwise. Even if we wanted it to be [otherwise], it would not be healthy for [a priest] to have that desire.

329. Cristofer: *What changes when you become a bishop in terms of leadership? Is it all the same?*

330. Bishop Olmsted: Well, there's only one sacrament of Holy Orders. So, there's obviously a very close link between the diaconate, and especially being a priest or bishop. Leadership, in particular, is very much a part of the priesthood and becoming a bishop.

331. The office of the bishop is built around teaching, sanctifying, and governing. All of those require that the bishop exercise leadership. He does that by recognizing that Jesus wants to, through him, exercise his leadership among others. There's a constant need for the bishop to be mindful of those three primary duties and to ask for the grace, the courage, the wisdom, and the collaborators needed in order to exercise leadership in this time and diocese where he is the bishop.

332. Cristofer: *Great leaders are often found to be surrounded by great advisors. Can you talk a little bit about what you look for in the staff that have supported you? What qualities, what skills? Do you have any best practices you can share regarding communicating and working with advisory boards?*

333. Bishop Olmsted: As a bishop, it is the Lord who determines whom and where we shall serve. The priests, deacons, and lay faithful with whom we work closely are also part of God's providence. From among them, most of a bishop's leaders come.

334. Before deciding whom to choose, I sought counsel from among those who knew best the challenges and opportunities we were facing and who might be most helpful in addressing those. Qualities I looked for were fidelity to Christ and the Catholic Faith, trustworthiness, leadership ability, basic skills that would be needed and a capacity to collaborate well with others.

335. These include, above all, the Presbyteral Council and Diocesan Finance Council. The Presbyteral Council should be made up of priests of various ages, pastoral experience, theological, pastoral, and canonical expertise, language and cultural backgrounds and so forth. The Diocesan Finance Council is made up primarily of lay people coming from a variety of professions, such as real estate, banking, law, investments, insurance, and so forth.

336. Close collaborators can be quite helpful in the search for and final selection of new personnel.

337. Cristofer: *One of the challenges of being a leader is making tough decisions. You certainly have been called to do that while serving in Phoenix. Can you talk a little about the approach you take in resolving challenging situations? How have the principles of Catholic Social Teaching helped?*

338. Bishop Olmsted: Decision making greatly impacts the future of a local Church, its schools, parishes, charitable organizations, and relations with local civic and cultural leaders and organizations. When facing tough decisions, the first priority is to get to know well the problems that must be addressed, the primary goals to be achieved, and what hindrances and difficulties will need to be dealt with. A good understanding of Catholic Social Teaching is needed for sound decisions and a personal commitment to the moral and theological truths of our Faith.

339. Cristofer: *Managing growth is another common challenge for leadership that requires decisions about priorities and resource allocations. During your tenure as Bishop of Phoenix, new schools have been built, university programs started, Newman Centers expanded, and the JPII Resource Center developed. What leadership skills or attributes were most useful to you in deciding what to pursue and not to pursue, and when?*

340. Bishop Olmsted: In a fast-growing diocese like Phoenix, institutions for Catholic Education, Evangelization, Charitable and Pastoral services, and so forth require good strategic planning. Key partners in addressing these challenges are the Diocesan Finance Council, Diocesan School Board, Presbyteral Council, Pastors of parishes, leaders of educational, cultural and charitable organizations such as Knights of Columbus, St. Vincent de Paul Society, Institutions of Higher Education, and so forth. When managing growth and making strategic plans, members of the Catholic lay faithful fulfill pivotal roles.

341. Cristofer: *Several Religious groups have also come to the diocese during your tenure and even built new monasteries. Can you tell us a little about the importance of that?*

342. Bishop Olmsted: Consecrated Life, Religious Sisters, Brothers, and clergy play vital roles in the mission of the Church. The Church suffers a great spiritual, evangelical, and educational poverty without them. Many newly arrived immigrants can only be adequately served when we have Sisters, Brothers, Priests and Deacons who understand their culture and speak their language. It is the role of the bishop to invite these consecrated persons to come and serve in the local Church. The Holy Spirit also stirs up in the hearts of people various charisms to meet the emerging needs and opportunities.

343. Cristofer: *The Phoenix Diocese is diverse – with multiple languages, cultures (Hispanic, Native American, etc.) and even different rites within the Catholic Church. Can you talk a little about some of the highlights?*

344. Bishop Olmsted: The Catholic Church carries on the mission of Jesus, the Redeemer and Light of the world. The gifts and charisms of the Holy Spirit are given to peoples of all languages, cultures and liturgical traditions. When you live in a large city receiving immigrants from around the world, this rich mixture of people and traditions is brought together locally by God's providence.

345. Constantly, the bishop and his collaborators must seek out the newly arrived men, women and children who come from cultures not previously found in our area; then, make efforts to discover and invite Religious, clergy and trained lay faithful who can meet some of their needs.

346. Bishops of the Latin Rite in America also have a duty to assist newly arrived Catholics of Eastern Catholic Churches to have their own clergy and Religious to assist them. This has been a constant and still growing need in Arizona. Some examples include Catholics of the Syro-Malabar Church coming from India, the Chaldean Church and the Syriac Catholic Churches, and many more.

347. Cristofer: *As bishop, you had to wear many hats – to your priests, you were brother and father, etc. etc. Most Catholic lay leaders also have to wear many hats – parent, spouse, employee, volunteer, servant, etc. etc. Please talk about how you can keep the various roles "straight" and be who you need to be in various moments without hypocrisy, etc.*

65

348. Bishop Olmsted: Be more concerned about "who you are" than about "what you do." Wholesome relationships and good friends flow from a virtuous "habit of being." Be a faithful friend. Cultivate friends who love you enough to tell you what you need to hear, not what you want to hear.

349. Cristofer: *I know you're very familiar with Opus Dei and the teachings of St. Josemaria. Can you tell me a little bit about what you discovered through your doctoral dissertation studies and the role of the laity?*

350. Bishop Olmsted: I wrote my doctoral dissertation on the secularity of secular institutes. A secular institute is an institute of consecrated life. People make promises of poverty, chastity, and obedience, but they remain in the world for the sake of the world. And there, they are in a very close collaboration with lay people who are consecrated through baptism, but don't have the further vow of poverty, chastity, and obedience, or the call to celibacy and virginity.

351. There were many places where you could not publicly be known as being religious, like in totalitarian governments. After the fall of the Iron Curtain, I think St. John Paul II was convinced that we were moving in the West to a lack of freedom and a hegemony of forces within society, which would make it really difficult to live one's Faith, like what they had experienced under communism. Totalitarianism, the whole of relativism itself, can really reduce the kind of freedom that people feel and that they need to fulfill their vocations.

352. Cristofer: *What are some of the leadership lessons that you learned from St. John Paul II?*

353. Bishop Olmsted: He impacted my life so much!

354. Cristofer: *It's interesting that just bringing up his name brings a smile to your face.*

355. Bishop Olmsted: Yes. I was constantly inspired by him and his *Ecclesia in America - Encountering the Living Jesus Christ* (St. John Paul II 1999) and the paths there. Those would be key for me. And the fact that he articulated the tough truths of the Faith so clearly and so convincingly, the ones that contradicted the lies that the evil one had planted in society or even within the body of the Church itself. That's one of the things that struck me. He really felt called to do that because he saw the impact on a society under communism, especially Nazism, which tried to stop that [articulation of truth] from happening. He felt the leaders had to do that. His strong leadership with regard to the truths that need to be held up would be one [leadership lesson].

356. His strong conviction about the fact that lay people have a primary mission in the Church [would be another]. It's one that lay people do in the ordinary circumstances of their lives and in the profession or talents and gifts that God gives them; that's where they exercise their role. They often do it best when they are supported by others and when they look for ways to work with others - together. I saw how [St. John Paul II] did that himself. Imitating that often bore good fruit in my ministry, I think, as a bishop.

357. Cristofer: *Thank you. How about other influences? Are there other leaders that have inspired you, where you sought to find the wisdom that you needed as a bishop? I've often heard you quote St. Padre Pio, but there might be others whom I don't know who inspire you.*

358. Bishop Olmsted: Yes, [Venerable] Padre Kino. He really made great efforts to get to know the native peoples, work alongside them, and engage them in doing that. As did St. Junipero Serra. Junipero Serra was great at doing that before he ever came to California when he went up to the Sierra Gorda and was pastor of a church. All of the architecture there had a real Indian influence in terms of images and all. So, I learned a lot from those two.

359. St. Charles de Foucauld greatly impacted me because of his great belief that the adoration of the Eucharist had such power to transform our own hearts and to be a source of grace for those that we went to serve as well, like his seeking out the most forgotten people in society. He felt that he should look at a map and if there was any place in the world where there was one group of people who might never hear the name of Jesus unless he went there - that was where he should go. That was why he ended up going to the

southern part of the Sahara Desert, where they didn't know anything about Jesus.

360. That witness of seeking out those who might never hear [Jesus] name, and that link with the adoration which kept his heart always on fire with love for Jesus, that's where I got the Jesus Caritas symbol and those two words for my own model as a bishop. That was all from Charles de Foucauld; he would have a big impact on my life.

361. Cristofer: *Can you talk a little bit more about organizational memberships that were important to you after you became a priest and why?*

362. Bishop Olmsted: The organization that has had the biggest impact on my life is the Priestly Fraternity of Jesus Caritas, which assisted me to grow in brotherly love and daily witnessing to the Gospel with my brother priests. It prompted me to make personal commitments that have shaped my life and ministry, e.g., making an hour of Eucharistic Adoration every day in addition to the Liturgy of the Hours and daily Mass.

363. The Equestrian Order of the Holy Sepulchre has deepened my awareness of the mystery of the Cross of Christ and the unique witness to the Gospel of Christ made by Christians living in the Holy Land. It provides concrete programs and means of working for peace in the Middle East and supporting those suffering from tensions and hardships in that part of the world.

364. The Catholic Association for Latino Leadership (CALL), together with its founders Archbishop Jose Gomez and Archbishop Charles Chaput, have helped me to grow in my appreciation of the rich cultural and spiritual gifts of the Hispanic Community and provided many opportunities to collaborate closely with Hispanic Catholic leaders in the Church and society.

365. Cristofer: *Please tell me more about your involvement in founding the CALL.*

366. Bishop Olmsted: Shortly after I was named a bishop in Wichita, Archbishop Gomez was named an auxiliary bishop in Denver. I did not know him before, but I wanted to get to know him because it was a neighboring diocese. He invited me to come to a meeting about what eventually became the CALL. It was a meeting of Hispanic leaders with bishops and priests, but mostly bishops. As soon as I saw that, I said, this is definitely something I want to do. That's how I got to know him [Archbishop Gomez], through his inviting me to come to that. I already knew Archbishop Chaput as well, who was the archbishop [in Denver at that time].

367. The CALL immediately made sense, partly because I saw St. John Paul II's example. I knew that we needed leadership among our immigrant communities, leadership from those among them who have a chance to be good leaders in society. They could just fade in as if they weren't Hispanic, or they could be good examples for their brothers and sisters who were Hispanic and really built up something there. Archbishop Gomez articulated it much better than I could, but standing side by side, you could get more sense of how this could impact people.

368. Cristofer: *I think everybody now that is a practicing Catholic or involved in the leadership of the Church in the United States will identify with this. By now, the Hispanic community is an important part of the Church in the United States. Many would say it's the future; it is the face of the future of the Church. When did you begin to see it? What does it actually mean that Latinos are the future of the Church?*

369. Bishop Olmsted: Well, we just look to see what the reality is. We don't try to force something on it. But what is happening? The fact is the Hispanic population is growing, largely through immigration to this country. A significant amount of that population is Catholic. Immigrants are always in a time when their Faith is challenged because they're in another country. They've got so many other things to do just to make a living. So, they need extra support, but if we give them that, they will impact the more recently arriving immigrants as well. So, it's a very fragile but very important area that we need to spend time on. The ones in that group who are leaders are given the grace and the opportunity to have a real impact.

370. Cristofer: *Thank you! People can talk about leadership for hours, but many struggle to define it. How would you define leadership?*

371. Bishop Olmsted: One of the things I think is needed for leadership is to articulate, be able to explain, and make a constant effort to be handing on the Gospel. Jesus' command, His great commission, is - Go, teach all nations, "baptizing them in the name of the Father, and of the Son, and of the Holy Spirit." I will be with you always, but go, teach (Matt. 28:19-20).

372. There's something in being witnesses to the truth, especially to the truth which is Jesus himself. That is a vital part of leadership because those words [go, teach] are not only for the apostles; they are for every member of the Church. I would put that at the heart of leadership.

373. The articulation is sometimes just in the ordinary circumstances of life; just putting into words as best I can something that this person needs to hear that they would not otherwise know or that they may think the opposite of because they've never heard anything other than the lies of the evil one.

374. Cristofer: *For many lay people, Catholic leaders are only found in the ranks of the clergy. Some lay people have trouble seeing themselves as leaders. The other common view is that lay Catholic leaders are those involved in activities or initiatives at the parish or diocesan level. The organization that you founded and that will publish this book promotes a different view of lay Catholic leadership. Can you speak to lay Catholic leadership for civil society?*

375. Bishop Olmsted: I very much agree that, too often, we thought of lay people as not having a major role in the Church. But from what I see happening today, a lot of the leadership that is really having an impact is being done by lay people.

376. I think of all those in this diocese who teach the Theology of the Body at the St. John Paul II Center. We have the witness of the impact that has on married couples, on those preparing for marriage, or being called to marriage. Also, all of those many [lay people] who teach in Spanish, in English, in Vietnamese and in other languages - the impact that has on other couples is just remarkable. Their whole lives and the witness of lay people to God's plan for marriage and Natural Family Planning is primary. It's much more convincing than I can give because they're speaking as witnesses; they're living this!

That is really badly needed in a society that doesn't understand marriage and is constantly doing things that are totally opposite of marriage and proposing things that twist around the notion of the dignity of each human person as a man or as a woman.

377. So, I really think this is the hour of the laity. I'm really convinced about that. I'm seeing a number of lay people, from yourself to people like Mike Phelan, to those who teach Natural Family Planning, and those involved in communications in our diocese. It's really bearing very good fruit. A lot of it we don't get to see in larger numbers, but the truth is like that. There's a humility connected with it often. It doesn't have to be noticed by others; it can still bear fruit.

378. **Cristofer:** *Thank you, Bishop. There are plenty of examples of Catholic leadership from the clergy, and we have a long list of saints that we know. But we do not know as many lay saints. Which are the first lay saints that come to mind for you?*

379. **Bishop Olmsted:** Saint Gianna Molla. Her great example as a wife, as a medical doctor, and as a mother - joyful in all of those vocations and freely giving her life for the sake of the child. So, she would be one that I think is very, very important. I am also struck by [Blessed] Carlo Acutis, a young Italian boy; his love for the Eucharist as a teenager is very powerful, I think.

380. There are a lot of people dying as martyrs these days in countries of conflict. So, I think we can never forget the martyrs because that witness, in many ways, touches hearts more than any other witness. I'm thinking of all those who are dying in countries like Ukraine, Nigeria, and other places. The large majority of them are lay people and I think the Lord is raising up some really great saints in that regard.

381. I think some of those speaking out in the media, against a media that tries to silence voices of truth and goodness, are a great blessing for us as well.

382. **Cristofer:** *You have a special devotion to St. Thomas More, who, like John the Baptist, gave his life to defend God and the Church's definition of marriage. In this age of claimed redefinition of*

marriage/gender fluidity, etc., what can we, on a practical level, learn from More in how we respond to this challenge?

383. Bishop Olmsted: St. Thomas More kept family life as a top priority in his life. No matter how busy he was, he took time to oversee the education and faith formation of his children. Living in an age that thinks it possible to "re-define marriage," keep in mind the example of Thomas More, who, even unto death, held that God's plan for marriage takes precedence over anyone else's plans, including an earthly king. Be prepared to give the reasons for your trust in God's plan.

384. Cristofer: *Please talk about the urgency and supreme calling to defend innocent life in all its stages. You were often found giving silent witness and courage to your flock standing outside clinics, etc. Please talk about your feelings on this subject and what compelled you as bishop to be on those sidewalks no matter the weather.*

385. Bishop Olmsted: The culture of death is built on cleverly concocted, false reasoning that has no foundation in truth. It is built on lies. When killing is proposed as a solution rather than a violation of human dignity, remember Jesus' words, "If you love me, you will keep my commandments" (John 14:15). When the Ten Commandments, especially "You shall not kill" and "You shall not commit adultery" (Deut. 5:17-18), are deliberately ignored, do not forget your duty and grace from God to stand up in defense of the most vulnerable among us, especially the unborn, and to live the virtue of chastity.

386. Cristofer: *Thank you, Bishop. I have a list of things that I think get neglected. This is one I wish I would hear more of from the pulpit - a clear call that we are all called to be saints. We talk about life, we talk about faith, we talk about leadership, but ultimately, it has to do with our identity, who we are as children of God and the purpose of our lives. Please share your thoughts on the importance of discovering this – our universal call to holiness, particularly for the lay people.*

387. Bishop Olmsted: I agree. Something happens within us when we become convinced that Jesus really called us to be His and draw close to His heart. "It was not you who chose me, but I chose you" (John

15:16). [Holiness happens] when those words become really true for us. The two words that need to come together are 'come' and 'go.' So, He chose us, and He calls us to himself first. That was true for the apostles and the other disciples, too. But then, at a certain point, He says, "Go… Make disciples of all nations" (Matt. 28:19). And all of that - is a call to holiness.

388. It's a call to Him because that's what holiness is. It's a union with Him. It's a communion with Him. The more we allow the grace of conversion that comes to us, the more we'll have a communion with Him. The solidarity that it brings about with others makes it fruitful.

389. But, if we forget that we're called to holiness, and we forget that it is possible to have a really deep loving relationship with Jesus, we are never going to accomplish anything. We can't do it on our own. We'll begin to think we can out of pride, or we'll be pouting and becoming even more turned in on ourselves.

390. Certainly, that sense that every human person was created to be a witness of Christ, to know Him, and to be a witness of His - that is vitally needed. Vitally needed. It is such a secularized society that just saying it is being counter-cultural in a really healthy way that the world needs.

391. So that call to holiness, the willingness to listen, to take it in and to be really convinced about it, and joyful that I have been called to do this - those are great blessings that the world needs. Lay people's witness is vitally needed for others to trust in that call.

TIMELINE OF
MOST REV. THOMAS J. OLMSTED

Birthday: January 21, 1947

Ordination to the priesthood: July 2, 1973

Ordained a bishop: April 20, 1999

1973-1976: First assignment as a priest: associate pastor, Cathedral of the Risen Christ, Lincoln, Nebraska

1976-1979: Doctoral Studies at the Gregorian University, Rome

1979-1988: Assistant at the Secretariat of State of the Holy See, and assistant spiritual director at Pontifical North American College, Rome

1989-1993: Pastor, St. Vincent de Paul Parish, Seward, Nebraska

1993-1997: Dean of Personal Formation at the Pontifical College Josephinum, Columbus, Ohio

1997-1999: Rector/President of the Pontifical College Josephinum

1999-2001: Coadjutor Bishop of the Diocese of Wichita, Kansas

1999-2007: USCCB Priestly Formation Committee

2000-2003: USCCB Consecrated Life Committee

2000-2003: Board of Directors, Catholic Legal Immigration Network, Inc.

2000-2003: USCCB Administrative Committee

2001-2003: Bishop of the Diocese of Wichita, Kansas

2003-2022: Bishop of the Diocese of Phoenix

2005-2008: Member, USCCB National Advisory Council

2008-2009: Apostolic Administrator of Diocese of Gallup

2008-2017: Member, USCCB Committee on Ecumenical and Inter-Religious Affairs

2009-Present: Founding Member, Catholic Association of Latino Leaders

2010-2011: Member, USCCB Missions Committee

2010-2017: Board of Trustees, The Catholic University of America

2011-2015: Ad Hoc Committee on Religious Liberty

2011-2015: First Vice-Chairman, Vox Clara Committee of the Congregation for Divine Worship

2011-2021: Board of Trustees, Saint John Vianney Theological Seminary

2011-2023: Episcopal Advisory Board, Augustine Institute, Denver

2011-Present: Episcopal Advisor to the US Conference of Secular Institutes

2011-Present: Board of Directors, Spitzer Center for Ethical Leadership

2011-Present: Board of Directors, Courage

2015-2019: Board of Governors of the Pontifical North American College

2015-2024: USCCB Pro-Life Committee Member

2018-2023: Appointed Apostolic Administrator of the Holy Protection of Mary Byzantine Catholic Eparchy of Phoenix. Seda Plena.

2018-Present: Cofounder and Ecclesiastical Advisor for Tepeyac Leadership Initiative

2022: Resignation submitted upon turning 75 years of age.

Adapted from The Roman Catholic Diocese of Phoenix Website. Accessed February 2, 2024. https://dphx.org/about/bishop-thomas-j-olmsted/

PUBLICATIONS OF
MOST REV. THOMAS J. OLMSTED

2021. *Veneremur Cernui – Down in Adoration Falling.* Apostolic Exhortation, The Roman Catholic Diocese of Phoenix. Accessed April 18, 2024. https://dphx.org/veneremur-cernui/.

2021. *O Sacred Feast.* Pastoral Letter, The Roman Catholic Diocese of Phoenix. Accessed April 18, 2024. https://dphx.org/o-sacred-feast-a-pastoral-letter-from-bishop-olmsted-to-all-the-faithful-of-the-diocese-of-phoenix/.

2020. *Pastoral Statement on USCCB "Open Wide Our Hearts: The Enduring Call to Love".* The Roman Catholic Diocese of Phoenix. Accessed April 18, 2024. https://dphx.org/a-pastoral-statement-from-bishop-olmsted-to-the-diocese-of-phoenix/.

2019. *Bishop Olmsted Expresses Sorrow Over Border Tragedy.* Accessed April 18, 2024. https://dphx.org/bishop-olmsted-expresses-sorrow-over-border-tragedy/.

2018. *Complete My Joy.* Phoenix: The Roman Catholic Diocese of Phoenix. Accessed April 18, 2024. https://family.dphx.org/.

2017. *Evangelizing through Catholic Schools.* Apostolic Letter, The Roman Catholic Diocese of Phoenix. https://dphx.org/evangelizing-through-catholic-schools/.

2016. *Catholics in the Public Square.* 4th. Charlotte: Saint Benedict Press.

2016. "Reflections: Amoris Laetitia, Pope Francis' Post-Synodal Apostolic Exhortation On Love in the Family." *The Catholic Sun.* The Roman Catholic Diocese of Phoenix. Accessed April 18, 2024. https://dphx.org/amoris-laetitia-the-joy-of-love/.

2015. *Into the Breach.* Apostolic Exhortation, The Roman Catholic Diocese of Phoenix. Accessed April 11, 2024. https://dphx.org/into-the-breach/.

2013. *Apostles of Mercy.* Pastoral Letter, The Roman Catholic Diocese of Phoenix. Accessed April 18, 2024. https://dphx.org/apostles-of-mercy/.

2012. "The Blessing of a Fruitful Life: Reflections on 'Humanae Vitae', the encyclical letter of Pope Paul VI on the Regulation of Birth." *The Catholic Sun.* The Roman Catholic Diocese of Phoenix. Accessed April 18, 2024. https://dphx.org/the-blessing-of-a-fruitful-life/.

2009. "Covenant of Love - Pastoral Letter." *The Catholic Sun.* The Roman Catholic Diocese of Phoenix. Accessed April 18, 2024. https://dphx.org/wp-content/uploads/2015/09/PL-Covenant-of-Love-Pastoral-080609.pdf.

2009. "Serving Truth in the University - A Pastoral Letter." *The Catholic Sun.* The Roman Catholic Diocese of Phoenix. Accessed April 18, 2024. https://dphx.org/wp-content/uploads/2015/09/PL-Serving-Truth-In-The-University-121709.pdf.

2006. "Why is Marriage Important to the Catholic Church? A Pastoral Statement of the Arizona Catholic Conference Bishops." *The Catholic Sun.* The Roman Catholic Diocese of Phoenix. Accessed April 18, 2024. https://dphx.org/wp-content/uploads/2015/09/PL-Marriage-Statement-030206.pdf.

2005. *Self-Giving Love, Reflections on 'Humanae Vitae', the encyclical letter of Pope Paul VI on the Regulation of Birth.* The Roman Catholic Diocese of Phoenix. Accessed April 18, 2024. https://dphx.org/self-giving-love-humanae-vitae/.

2005. *Gift from on High: Pastoral Letter on the Sacrament of Confirmation.* Pastoral Letter, The Roman Catholic Diocese of Phoenix. https://dphx.org/gift-from-on-high-pastoral-letter-on-the-sacrament-of-confirmation/.

2005. "You Welcomed Me: A Pastoral Letter on Migration Released on the Feast of Our Lady of Guadalupe." *The Catholic Sun.* The Roman Catholic Diocese of Phoenix. Accessed April 18, 2024. https://dphx.org/wp-content/uploads/2015/09/PL-You-Welcomed-Me-121505.pdf.

From The Roman Catholic Diocese of Phoenix Website. Accessed April 18, 2024. https://dphx.org/category/exhortations-letters-columns-olmsted/

REFERENCES

Boas, Sherry. 2019. *Laughter of Angels.* Caritas Press.

Boas, Sherry. 2011. *Until Lily.* Caritas Press.

CNA Staff. 2021. *Fatima visionary predicted 'final battle' would be over marriage, family.* Mexico City, 13 October. Accessed April 10, 2024. https://www.catholicnewsagency.com/news/34155/fatima-visionary-predicted-final-battle-would-be-over-marriage-family.

Day, Dorthy. 1963. *Loaves and Fishes.* Harper and Row.

Day, Dorthy. 1952. *The Long Loneliness.* Harper and Brothers.

García, J.D. Long . 2022. "Courageous prophet or anti-Francis culture warrior? The Bishop Olmsted I knew was simply a pastor." *America.* Accessed April 11, 2024. https://www.americamagazine.org/faith/2022/06/15/bishop-olmsted-phoenix-retirement-243161.

Houselander, Caryll. 1944. "Advent." In *The Reed of God.*

O'Brien, Michael D. 2010. *Island of the World.* Ignatius Press.

O'Brien, Michael D. 2011. *The Father's Tale.* Ignatius Press.

O'Connor, Flannery. 1979. *The Habit of Being.* Edited by Sally Fitzgerald. Farrar, Straus and Giroux.

Paul VI. 1968. *Humane Vitae.* Encyclical letter, Rome: The Holy See. Accessed April 10, 2024. https://www.vatican.va/content/paul-vi/en/encyclicals/documents/hf_p-vi_enc_25071968_humanae-vitae.html.

Philippe, Father Jacques. 2021. *Priestly Fatherhood, Treasure in Earthen Vessels.* Scepter Publishers.

Powers, Jessica. 1999. *The Selected Poetry of Jessica Powers.* ICS Publications.

Second Vatican Council. 1965. *Apostolicam Actuositatem - Decree on the Apostolate of the Laity.* The Holy See, 18 November. Accessed April 11, 2024. https://www.vatican.va/archive/hist_councils/ii_vatican_council/documents/vat-ii_decree_19651118_apostolicam-actuositatem_en.html.

Second Vatican Council. 1965. *Dei Verbum - Dogmatic Constitution on Divine Revelation.* The Holy See, 18 November. Accessed April 11, 2024. https://www.vatican.va/archive/hist_councils/ii_vatican_council/documents/vat-ii_const_19651118_dei-verbum_en.html.

Second Vatican Council. 1964. *Lumen Gentium - Dogmatic Constitution on the Church.* The Holy See, 21 November. Accessed April 11, 2024. https://www.vatican.va/archive/hist_councils/ii_vatican_council/documents/vat-ii_const_19641121_lumen-gentium_en.html.

Second Vatican Council. 1963. *Sacrosanctum Concilium - Constitution on the Sacred Liturgy.* The Holy See, 4 December. Accessed April 11, 2024. https://www.vatican.va/archive/hist_councils/ii_vatican_council/documents/vat-ii_const_19631204_sacrosanctum-concilium_en.html.

St. Catherine of Siena. 1991. *Dialogue of St. Catherine of Siena.* Tan Books.

St. John Paul II. 1999. *Ecclesia in America - On the Encounter with the Living Jesus Christ.* Apostolic Exhortation, The Holy See. Accessed April 10, 2024. https://www.vatican.va/content/john-paul-ii/en/apost_exhortations/documents/hf_jp-ii_exh_22011999_ecclesia-in-america.html.

St. John Paul II. 1979. *Homily of His Holiness John Paul II.* Eucharistic Celebration, Mexico, Basilica of Guadalupe: The Holy See. Accessed April 11, 2024. https://www.vatican.va/content/john-paul-ii/en/homilies/1979/documents/hf_jp-ii_hom_19790127_messico-guadalupe.html.

St. John Paul II. 1986. *Homily of John Paul II.* Perth: The Holy See, para. 4. Accessed April 10, 2024. https://www.vatican.va/content/john-paul-ii/en/homilies/1986/documents/hf_jp-ii_hom_19861130_perth-australia.html.

St. John Paul II. 1979. *Redemptor Hominis.* Encyclical Letter, Rome: The Holy See, para. 10. Accessed April 11, 2024. https://www.vatican.va/content/john-paul-ii/en/encyclicals/documents/hf_jp-ii_enc_04031979_redemptor-hominis.html.

St. Joseph Maronite Catholic Church in Phoenix, Arizona. 2016. *She Came And Prayed Asking St. Sharbel To Cure Her.* 18 January. Accessed April 11, 2024. https://stjosephphoenix.org/st-sharbel/miracles/she-came-and-prayed-asking-st-sharbel-to-cure-her.

The Holy See. 2019. *Catechism of the Catholic Church.* 2nd. United States Conference of Catholic Bishops. Accessed April 11, 2024. https://www.usccb.org/sites/default/files/flipbooks/catechism/.

Zucarelli, Paul. 2018. *Faith Understood: An Ordinary Man's Journey to the Presence of God.* Zucarelli Family Faith Charitable Trust.

2022. *The Quiet Girl.* Directed by Colm Bairéad. Performed by Carrie Crowley.

2023. *Sound of Freedom.* Directed by Alejandro Monteverde. Performed by Jim Caviezel.

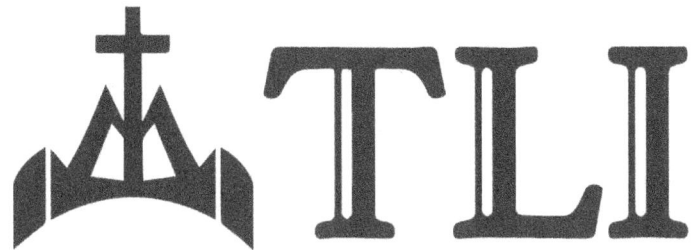

We hope you enjoyed this book.

Please consider supporting our efforts by learning about,
praying for, or financially supporting
Tepeyac Leadership, Inc.

Please visit:

TLIprogram.org
THLconference.org